500 Chess Questions Answered

Andrew Soltis

First published in the United Kingdom in 2021 by
Batsford
43 Great Ormond Street
London WC1N 3HZ
An imprint of Pavilion Books Company Ltd

ISBN: 9781849947121

A CIP catalogue record for this book is available from the British Library.

26 25 24 23 22 21
10 9 8 7 6 5 4 3 2 1

Reproduction by Rival Colour Ltd, UK
Printed and bound by CPI Books, Chatham, UK

This book can be ordered direct from the publisher at www.pavilionbooks.com, or try your local bookshop

Contents

Foreword

This is a book for people who are discovering how hard it is to get better at chess. They are learning more. But they are also learning there is much more to learn.

They have scanned Web sites and blogs, browsed books and watched videos. But for every question these resources answer, they have more questions that go unanswered.

I've tried to answer the most often asked questions. Here is some advice before you start.

Don't try to swallow too much in one sitting. A dozen questions may be a lot to absorb. Chess ideas take a while to sink in.

But feel free to open this book on any page when you have a spare moment. Improving is incremental. Allow yourself to take the increments.

For many of the questions and answers, you won't need a board and pieces or a computer. Even for the questions that have diagrams and move analysis, you may benefit by reading the text first and coming back to the page later – when you have time to think about it again and you can see more clearly what the moves mean.

Finally, I'd like to thank my wife, Marcy, and others who helped with this book, including Andras, Debra, Kevin and Lubosh.

Andrew Soltis
New York 2021

Chapter One: **Talent**

1. Do I need natural talent to play chess?

No – and there is some doubt natural chess talent exists.

There have been many attempts to detect it. But the results are inconclusive. Perhaps the most famous aptitude tests were created by a Czech scientist, Pavel Cerny, to study his country's young players.

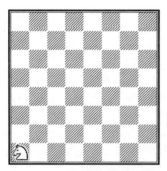

Knight tour to b1

In this first version, he asked subjects to figure out how to get the knight to b1 in the fewest moves. Simple enough.

Once they did that, he asked them to get it from b1 to c1. The test continued as the subjects had to reach d1, then e1 and so on to h1.

Once the first rank was done, the knight had to reach a2, then b2, c2 and all the second-rank squares. This was followed by the third-rank squares, and so on until the knight had gotten to h8. The subjects were asked to do it as quickly as they could.

Cerny devised a second, more challenging version of his test. He added four Black pawns.

Knight tour to h8

The knight had to perform the same task but without capturing a pawn or landing on a square that allowed a pawn to capture it.

Most experienced players can solve the second version in less than ten minutes.

2. So doing it quickly determines whether you are born with talent?

Not that alone. That is controversial.

One of the subjects, Lubos Kavalek, performed the second task in less than four minutes. He later became a grandmaster. But he called Cerny's project "a stupid test."

What seems clearer is this: If you take the tests a second time and perform the tasks faster than the first time, you have the talent *to learn chess*.

This confirms a long-held belief of chess teachers: The best gauge of ability is how well you can absorb what you study and then apply it.

Lothar Schmid, a grandmaster and world correspondence chess champion, said:

"You can tell if you have talent if you understand what a weak square is, what development really means. If a young player can grasp these things quickly then he has talent."

3. But what about chess prodigies? They must be born with talent.

A Hungarian psychologist did not believe natural talent existed and realized there was one way to prove it: By turning his children into prodigies.

After studying the biographies of hundreds of great thinkers, he concluded they were not born geniuses. Rather, they had intensely studied a specialized subject when they were young.

The psychologist, László Polgar, tried to do this with his three young daughters. They became the most famous female prodigies in chess history.

And, by the way, the term "chess prodigy" is obsolete.

It made sense when Bobby Fischer became a grandmaster at 15 because he was so unique. But since Fischer did that, more than three generations ago, there have been more than 40 youngsters who earned the grandmaster title at an earlier age. The rarity of a "chess prodigy" has disappeared.

4. *Do you have to be smart to play chess well?*

There are very good players who have normal IQs. And there are very bright people who are terrible at chess. Bill Gates was mated by Magnus Carlsen in 12 seconds.

Gates – Carlsen
London 2014

1 e4 ♘c6 2 ♘f3 d5 3 ♗d3 ♘f6 4 exd5 ♕xd5 5 ♘c3 ♕h5 6 0-0 ♗g4 7 h3? ♘e5?! 8 hxg4 ♘fxg4

White to move

The world chess champion is bluffing a billionaire, with a threat of 9...♘xf3+ and 10...♕h2.

Gates would have been winning after 9 ♖e1!.

But the game ended with **9 ♘xe5?? ♕h2 mate**.

Some great players showed flashes of brilliance long before they mastered chess. Mikhail Tal, a future world champion, could multiply three-figure digits when he was 5. But many other masters showed no particular gifts when growing up.

5. *What personality traits make someone a good chess player?*

Masters often say it takes the ability to concentrate, the capacity to work and strong willpower.

Once you begin to compete in tournaments, two other qualities – self-confidence and honesty – are valuable.

But there is one attribute you need to get started.

6. *What is that?*

Curiosity.

An extreme example was featured early in the TV series *The Queen's Gambit*. Some viewers questioned how Beth Harmon, the main character, could be so obsessed with chess that she could not sleep. She visualized pieces on the ceiling of her bedroom instead.

László Polgar, that Hungarian psychologist, recalled how one night he found his daughter Sophia in the family bathroom, with the light on and a chessboard in her lap. She was fascinated by a position and her curiosity would not let go.

"Sophia, leave the pieces alone," he said.

"Daddy, they won't leave me alone!" she replied.

You don't need insomnia-inducing curiosity to play well. But you need to be curious to keep learning.

7. *How does self-confidence and honesty fit in?*

You need self-confidence to overcome doubts when you choose a move. You need to be honest with yourself to recognize your chess weaknesses when you make bad moves. Then you can correct them.

8. *You didn't mention memory. Is there a lot to memorize in chess?*

Yes, and it is very important – if you hope to become world champion. But if you just want to become a good player, memory is not very important.

You will need to memorize several opening moves, some common middlegame patterns and a few basic endgame positions.

But there have been several great players who had a poor memory. Richard Réti, one of the most profound chess thinkers of the 20th century, was notoriously absent-minded and regularly lost his briefcase.

A 21st century world champion, Vishy Anand, said his memory helped him early in his chess career – because he used it to pass school tests without doing a lot of homework. This saved him time to study chess instead.

9. *Does pure rote learning help?*

Masters say no. Yet they spend hours before a game memorizing dozens of opening moves.

Rote learning of certain chess material helps. You can master some basic endgame positions, for example, the way you master the multiplication table.

But there is a limit to what you can retain.

There have been young players who memorized dozens of tactical patterns. They could solve a "White to move and win" position.

Yet they did not fully understand the position. When shown the same position with the board reversed they could not find the same win.

White to move and win

This is the finish to one of the most famous games ever played, a brilliancy by the American superstar Paul Morphy. But it is usually presented with the White pieces at the bottom and the Black ones at the top.

The player who can solve it in the original form but not in this one has wasted his time memorizing. (Morphy ended the game with 16 ♕b8+! ♘xb8 17 ♖d8 mate.)

10. How long will it take me to become good at chess?

If you take chess seriously for two months, studying when you can, you should be able to beat an opponent who doesn't study at all.

11. How long will it take to become very good?

Very good should take years. So does being able to speak Mandarin fluently, play a Chopin piano concerto or perform any difficult skill.

Here's a very rough estimate: It typically takes a player seven or eight years to reach about 90 percent of his chess potential.

Magnus Carlsen learned how the chess pieces move when he was 5. He didn't study the game until he had an incentive – to beat his older sister. But once he took the game seriously he reached grandmaster strength in eight years.

12. What can I accomplish if I start later in life?

Chess is easiest to learn when you are young, your mind is most pliable and you have plenty of free time to spend on a board game.

Psychologist Anders Ericsson cited the Polgar sisters in explaining his theory that people can master a subject after at least 10,000 hours of "deliberate practice." You are not likely to have that many hours and that much productive studying later in life.

Yet many great players – and many more who became merely good players – started later than the Polgars. Akiba Rubinstein did not know how the pieces move until he was 14. Leonid Stein became a master at 24. Both men eventually became candidates for the world championship.

13. Can a late start in chess be helpful?

Yes, there is less chance of burnout.

There are youngsters who learned to play at six and won trophies in scholastic events four years later. But they never got much beyond what they knew at 10 and gave up chess a few years later.

A late start may also allow you to maintain enthusiasm longer.

"The sooner you start, the quicker you lose your interest or ambition," said Lajos Portisch. He got his first chess set when he was 12, played in his national championship six years later and remained in the world's elite for more than 30 years.

14. Are there any other qualities of a good player that aren't obvious?

Yes, the ability to get over a loss. You are going to lose hundreds of games before you become good at chess. You can't let them haunt you.

Sunil Weeramantry was an accomplished chess teacher before he taught his two sons to play. He recalled how his younger son, future star Hikaru Nakamura, reacted after this game.

Becerra – Nakamura

US Chess League 2009

1 e4 c5 2 ♘f3 ♘f6 3 e5 ♘d5 4 ♘c3 e6 5 ♘xd5 exd5 6 d4 ♘c6 7 dxc5 ♗xc5 8 ♕xd5 d6 9 ♗c4 ♕e7? 10 ♗g5! f6 11 0-0-0!

Now 11...fxg5 12 exd6 is very bad and so is 11...♘xe5 12 ♘xe5 dxe5 13 ♗b5+.

Play continued **11...dxe5 12 &he1**.

Black to move

This is what a big lead in development looks like. It generates threats such as 13 &xe5! &xe5 14 &xe5! &xe5 15 &d8 mate.

Black looked at the lost 12...fxg5 13 &xe5! and the dismal 12...&e6 13 &xe6 &xe6 14 &xe6 fxg5 15 &xe5. He decided to resign.

"Do you think he was upset?" Weeramantry recalled. "He just laughed and said it won't happen again."

You won't learn something from every game you play. The most meaningful lessons may come in the games that leave you saying to yourself "It won't happen again." Appreciating those games is one of the elements of true chess talent.

Chapter Two: **Material**

15. *What is "material" and why do we call it that?*

It means the pieces and pawns. We probably adopted the term from the French *matériel*, meaning military equipment.

Like many technical terms in chess it is a bit clumsy but so widely used it would be impossible to change now.

16. *When does a material advantage matter most?*

In the endgame. Just one extra pawn may be enough to win then.

But that is only a minor, potential factor in the opening. A material edge gradually grows in significance as the game goes on.

17. *Every beginners' book I've seen has a chart with numerical values of the pieces. How important is it?*

Very important – if you are a beginner.

It is easier to understand if you think of it as a chart of *exchange* values. It is the shorthand way of learning whether giving up one piece for another is a favorable, unfavorable or a balanced transaction.

A typical chart tells you a queen is worth ten points, a rook is worth five, a knight or bishop is worth three and a pawn is worth one.

This is useful to a beginner wondering if he can afford to give up his bishop for a knight, for example. But the real value of a piece depends on whether it can act like it should.

A bishop that can't act like a bishop – because it is severely restricted in movement – is not worth a knight. It is sometimes derided as "a big pawn."

18. *A queen can move like a rook and a bishop. Why is it worth more than having those two pieces?*

This is one of the first difficult concepts for a beginner. There are two conflicting ways of evaluating material.

The first is to judge a piece's ability to perform tasks on its own.

Most tactics are based on attacking two targets at once. The queen is far better than any other piece at making such a double attack.

White to move and win

White can capture the rook with **1 ♕d8+, 2 ♕d3+** and **3 ♕xb5**.

The queen moved like three pieces. The first move was that of a dark-squared bishop. The second was like a rook. The third was that of a light-squared bishop.

However, if it was Black's move in the diagram, neither side should win.

19. Why?

Because of that second way of evaluating material:

When two or more pieces cooperate, they increase in value. The sum is greater than the separate parts.

Black can play **1...♖g5!** and threaten ...♖xg2+ or ...♗xg2.

White can defend g2 with 2 g3. But he cannot win because Black's pieces also cooperate in defense. They can protect one another: Draw.

20. How often should I think about that chart during a game?

Rarely, once you've graduated from the ranks of beginner.

As you gain experience, the potential exchanges – such as a queen for two rooks – become as embedded in your consciousness as the alphabet.

You won't need the chart because other trades are somewhat rare. Even if you play 1,000 games, you will probably never need to know that a rook is worth five pawns, for example.

21. I know a king can't be exchanged. But how powerful is it?

More than most players know. One of the secrets of good endgame players is understanding that a king's offensive power is closest to that of a rook.

The king and rook are "natural enemies in the endgame," endgame composer Robert Burger said.

A rook can easily stop a passed pawn if its only support is a minor piece. But a rook has to play exactly to stop a pawn if it is near a king.

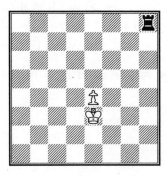

Black to move

White would make progress by advancing the pawn. For example, after 1...♖h4 2 ♔d4, with the idea of 3 ♔d5 and 4 e5.

But **1...♖e8!** thwarts him, 2 ♔d4 ♖d8+ 3 ♔c4 ♖e8! 4 ♔d5 ♖d8+.

The king/rook rivalry is unique and only matters in endgames.

22. Are there "best" squares for pieces?

Not squares but areas of the board.

The most important squares are usually in the center. Since the knight is a short-range piece, it does its best work in or near those center squares.

The rook and bishop are long-range pieces. They perform best when they are near the edges of the board because of a natural principle of chess: The stronger the piece, the more it is vulnerable to capture by a weaker piece.

As a result, rooks rarely occupy center squares until the endgame. Bishops often operate best from a near-edge square. A common example is ♗g2 by White after 1 ♘f3 and 2 g3.

A good formation

15

Note how well protected White's pieces and pawns are – while they control central squares: d4 and e5 by his knight, e3 by the f2-pawn and e4 and d5 by the bishop, once the knight moves.

The two remaining pieces to consider are the queen, a long-range piece, and the king, a short-range one. Both usually perform well in the center. But they are so valuable that they are kept protectively distant from it before the endgame.

23. Do the pieces change in value during a game?

This is another of the hardest of concepts to appreciate. They don't change much in *exchange* value. But they grow or decline in *offensive power.*

The knight is at its peak power in the opening and is the only piece that declines in strength. The rooks and bishops become stronger because the pawns that obstruct them are gradually captured.

Chess has a lot of maxims and one of them is "The future belongs to he who owns the bishops."

24. When is that future?

Computer analyses of hundreds of thousands of games have determined that the knight is superior to the bishop when each side has five or more pawns.

That's a generalization, of course, and it's not something you need to remember. But it is worth knowing that a bishop almost always gets better as the game goes on.

The same for a rook. It plays a minor role in the opening, joins the cast in the middlegame and assumes a leading role in a typical endgame.

25. What does that mean for me?

The best takeaway is: A rook is only worth its chart value when it can play like a rook.

Without open files to use, a rook may not play as well as a minor piece.

Novices often discover this in games that begin something like **1 e4 e5 2 ♘f3 ♘c6 3 ♗c4 ♗c5 4 ♘c3 ♘f6.**

They can go astray with **5 ♘g5 0-0 6 ♘xf7? ♖xf7 7 ♗xf7+ ♔xf7.**

White to move

According to the chart, material is equal.

The missing White pieces are his bishop (three points) and knight (three). That totals six points, the same as the missing Black rook (five) and pawn (one).

But White's extra rook won't get to make itself felt for a while. Black's minor pieces will, for example, after **8 d3 d6 9 0-0 ♗g4!**.

The game can draw to an early close after **10 ♕e1? ♘d4!**, threatening ...♘xc2. Then **11 ♕d2 ♕d7**.

White to move

Black could win in a few moves by using his two extra minor pieces, **12 b3 h6 13 ♗b2? ♘f3+! 14 gxf3 ♗xf3** and mate after ...♕g4 or ...♕h3-g2.

26. I know the stronger pieces are good at capturing. Is there anything else they do especially well?

They are splendid at restricting.

Here is an example of how a minor material advantage is decisive. White wins if he can capture the knight or the pawn. The key is restricting the knight.

Carlsen – Nakamura

Paris 2017

White to move

After **86 ♔f4!,** the king threatens to trap the knight with 87 ♔e3! and 88 ♔f2.

His rook needs only to restrict. For example, 86...♘c2+ 87 ♔e5! ♘g1 88 ♔e4! ♔g7 89 ♖h4!.

The game would end soon after 89...♔f6 90 ♔e3 and ♔f2.

Or after 89...♘e2 90 ♔d3 ♘c1+ 91 ♔c2 ♘e2 92 ♔d2.

This restricting technique has been known for more than a millennium. When the great endgame analyst Yuri Averbakh wrote the definitive analysis of K+R-versus-K+N, he cited a study by a ninth-century writer.

27. How come the knight and bishop are so close in value?

This is a happy accident that makes the nuances of modern chess possible.

The oldest surviving game with our rules began **1 e4 d5 2 exd5 ♕xd5 3 ♘c3 ♕d8 4 ♗c4 ♘f6 5 ♘f3 ♗g4.**

Both players overlooked the combination 6 ♗xf7+! ♔xf7 7 ♘e5+ and ♘xg4.

But what is significant is they both appreciated **6 h3.**

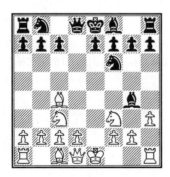

Black to move

Under the rules widely accepted before 1500, a bishop was a very weak piece, only slightly better than a pawn.

But under the new rules, a bishop and knight were suddenly roughly equal. Therefore, it made sense for White to encourage 6...♗xf3 and for Black to make that trade. After 7 ♕xf3 the winning chances were nearly even.

28. Don't masters prefer bishops?

Yes. Siegbert Tarrasch, a world-class player at the turn of the 20th century, favored them so much he said when you give up a knight for a bishop you have "won the minor exchange."

But another maxim states that while the bishop is stronger, "the knight is more clever."

Its ability to hop over friendly and enemy pieces and pawns gives it a special quality that even masters can find tricky, especially in speed chess.

"In blitz, the knight is stronger than the bishop," Grandmaster Vlastimil Hort said.

Gelfand – Kramnik

Internet 2020

White to move

White is close to a winning advantage. But he cannot play 47 ♗xc6 because of 47...♘c4+! and ...♘xd2.

He chose **47 ♔c5??**.

After **47...♘a5!** he realized he was lost. Both 48...♘xb7+ and the forking 48...♘b3+! were threatened.

Whether a knight is better than a bishop typically depends on where the pawns are. The bishop is the piece that varies most in value depending on pawn structure. A knight is frequently much better than a "bad bishop."

29. How bad is bad?

A really bad bishop may have no good moves at all. This happens most often when its own pawns do the limiting.

Caruana – Dominguez

Internet 2020

White to move

A bad bishop usually remains bad until the pawn structure changes. It will not change here.

After 82 ♗e3 ♔f5, for example, White must lose after 83...♔e4 or 83...♘xe3 84 ♔xe3 ♔g4 and ...♔xh4.

White resigned when he saw that and also 82 ♔f3 ♔f5!.

Of course, rooks, knights and the queen can also be poorly placed. But it is usually temporary.

Bishops influence the evaluation of a position more than any other piece. They can improve one player's chances significantly when he has "the two bishops."

30. Doesn't each player have two bishops when the game begins?

Yes, but a player no longer has them if he trades a bishop for knight. Then his opponent is said to have a "two-bishop advantage."

This becomes a significant advantage if there is a second knight-for-bishop trade. Then one player is left with two knights and the other has two bishops.

31. If neither player has a bad bishop, why do bishops matter?

That brings up a third way of evaluating material, the ability to attack targets.

If you have only one bishop, your opponent can put most of his pieces and pawns on squares of the other color.

Your bishop will have little to attack. It may be able to land on 32 squares. But the other 32 squares matter more.

32. What can pawns do besides promote to queens?

A pawn is the board's best defender, best blockader and also the best at driving away enemy pieces.

Black to move

White's knight is safe because of his pawns:

The pawn at c4 shields it from the rook. The pawn at b2 ensures that 1...♗xc3 is just a trade of pieces (2 bxc3). The pawn at d3 supports the c4-pawn.

But if the bishop were replaced on d4 by a Black pawn, it would threaten the more valuable knight and drive it away.

33. You said pieces increase in power when they cooperate. Which pieces cooperate best?

A queen works well with a knight, less so with a bishop. In an endgame with no other pieces, a queen and knight is often superior to a queen and bishop.

A rook coordinates better with a bishop than with a knight. In an extreme case with no pawns, a player with a king, rook and bishop would have good winning chances against an opponent with a king and rook.

But if the bishop is replaced by a knight, the winning chances are much less.

34. I've heard that when the two sides have bishops of opposite color it makes the position drawish. True?

Half true. The true part usually happens in an endgame.

You can have two or more extra pawns then and not have any real winning chances.

Harikrishna – Vachier-Lagrave

Wijk aan Zee 2021

White to move

White cannot make progress because he cannot create a passed kingside pawn or break the blockade on the queenside.

He agreed to a draw after **57 ♗c2 ♗b2 58 ♔e6 ♗c3 59 ♔d5 ♗d2 60 ♗d3 ♗c3 61 ♔e6 ♗b2 62 ♔d5 ♗c3 63 ♗e2 ♗d2 64 ♔e4**.

But if the White bishop were on virtually any dark square, winning would be fairly easy.

It would attack and then capture the f6-pawn. That dooms the g5-pawn and permits White to push his kingside pawns to promotion.

35. What is the part about bishops of opposite color that is untrue?

A position is not drawish when it is in a middlegame with few minor pieces.

Then you can attack enemy targets that are on squares of the color of your bishop. Your opponent's bishop cannot defend those squares. Nor can he offer a trade of bishops.

Donchenko – Firouzja

Wijk aan Zee 2021

Black to move

White is two pawns ahead. Once again the extra pawns don't matter. But this time it is for a very different reason.

Black's bishop helps make White vulnerable on light squares such as b1 and g2. White's bishop cannot defend those squares or trade itself for Black's bishop.

Play went **33...♖ab8! 34 ♕a2 ♖b1+! 35 ♖f1 ♖cb8 36 ♕f2 ♖xf1+ 37 ♔xf1 ♖b1+ 38 ♔e2 ♕b8!**.

The threat of 39...♕b5+!, on another light square, was decisive.

White resigned soon after **39 ♕f4 ♕b5+!**.

White to move

Because of 40 ♔f2 ♕f1+ 41 ♔g3 ♕xg2+ 42 ♔h4 ♖h1! 43 ♕g3 ♖xh3+!.

Having the better of the opposite-colored bishops may be considered a material advantage. Some masters rate it at roughly half a pawn.

36. How can you have half a pawn?

You can't saw one in half. But it helps to think of a fractional pawn when making common transactions.

If a transaction isn't quite equal, you need something else as compensation to balance it.

This is a somewhat sophisticated concept and you don't need to know it until you are more experienced.

37. But I'm curious. What are those transactions?

One is when a player gives up the Exchange, his rook for an enemy bishop or knight.

If he gets one pawn in return, it is insufficient compensation. If he gets two pawns, it is more than enough. In between is a pawn and a half.

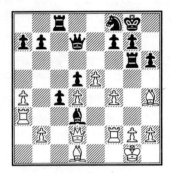

Duda – Ding Liren

Internet 2021

White to move

After **27 ℤxd3 cxd3** White will win the d3-pawn.

But that is not quite enough in a purely material sense. Some computers rate 27 ℤxd3 as the fifth best move in the position.

But it was a good sacrifice. Play continued **28 f5 ℤgc6 29 ♕xd3.**

The equation was balanced by other factors.

Black to move

White had two excellent bishops. Even though Black's rooks commanded an open file, their punching power was limited by the bishops, **29...ℤc1 30 ℤf1 ℤ8c4 31 ♗e1** and ♗d2.

In addition, White's e- and f-pawns can wreak havoc on the kingside if allowed to advance. Black soon felt compelled to return the Exchange for a pawn. He lost the endgame.

In other words, White managed to balance the sacrifice transaction by getting another kind of compensation.

And he did it without sawing a pawn in half.

Chapter Three: Choosing a Move

38. *Would a master always find a better move than the one I do?*

He will in many, if not most, positions that arise in your game.

But you play the best move a lot more often than you think.

When Garry Kasparov reviewed the games of the 2014 World Championship match, he said 70 percent of the moves could have been made "by any competent player."

Let's see some of them:

Anand – Carlsen

World Championship match 2014, first game

Black to move

As the middlegame began, the two players made a series of understandable moves. How many might you choose?

17...♛d6 (This threatens the f4-pawn.)

18 ♕d4 (This defends it.)

18...♖ad8 (There was no better square to develop this rook.)

19 ♗e6! (This protects the d5-pawn.)

19...♛b6! (A trade of queens helps Black.)

20 ♕d2 (White avoids it.)

20...♖d6 (Black prepares to eliminate the bishop with ...♘d8xe6!.)

White to move

21 ♖he1 (White protects it with his last undeveloped piece.)

21...♘d8! (Consistent with his last move)

22 f5 (More bishop protection)

22...♘xe6 (Consistent)

23 ♖xe6! (Better than 23 fxe6? ♖fd8!.)

23...♕c7+ (Defends the e7-pawn)

24 ♔b1 (The safest reply)

Let's review the seven White moves and seven Black moves since the first diagram.

Some were easy to understand. Some were harder. An average player might have played half of them. And he might choose alternatives that were nearly as good.

39. How should I start thinking about my next move?

Traditional advice tells us "Every move should have a purpose." So you begin by looking for moves backed by a reason.

Some will follow a general principle such as "Put rooks on open files." Others may set up a possible tactic. Or they may simply get greater use out of a poorly placed piece.

"I try to find a general idea," Boris Spassky said. "After that, when I think that this is the best move, then I start calculating."

40. How long should I think about my move?

After five minutes you should have some idea of what you would like to play. In many cases, you can come to a final decision in much less time.

In 2002 the world chess federation's championship match was won by an 18-year-old, Ruslan Ponomariev. He was making the most important moves of his life. But he never spent more than eight minutes on any move.

41. But shouldn't I take as much time as I can?

There is a danger in over-thinking.

This is what happens when you become frozen by doubts about the move you like. It is paralysis by analysis.

In chess, it is better to overcome your inhibitions, to be a Don Quixote rather than a Hamlet. Hamlets forfeit on time.

"If I study a position for an hour, then I'm usually going in loops and I'm probably not going to come up with something useful," Magnus Carlsen said.

"I usually know what I'm going to do after 10 seconds. The rest is double-checking."

42. Should I move quickly if I can?

In a clocked game, yes – if you feel good about the move you've chosen. Save your minutes for more difficult decisions.

But beware of "obvious moves." An obvious move is one that looks so right that it doesn't seem worthwhile to recheck it.

World Champion Mikhail Botvinnik was a mentor to another champion, Garry Kasparov. Kasparov had the natural impulse to make the first move that attracted him. Often, his choice was indeed the best move. But not always.

"Don't move," Botvinnik warned Kasparov. "Think first!"

The temptation to make an obvious move is so strong that some of the greatest players in history took extreme precautions. Siegbert Tarrasch and Vasily Smyslov occasionally sat on their hands – literally.

43. How important is it to find the best move every time?

You should *try* to play the best move. But there are two schools of thought about how hard you should try.

Kasparov said his great rival Anatoly Karpov had one outstanding attribute: Karpov did not agonize over finding the best move. In this practical way, he rarely ran short of time and made bad moves.

Kasparov added that Karpov's strongest point was also his weakest: He settled for second-best moves too often. Considering that Karpov was world champion for 10 years, his second-best moves were pretty good.

44. *Is there always a best move?*

Before computers, we believed the answer was "Yes." But engines have shown us that in many positions the answer is "No."

And in many others, the difference between best and second-best – or third best – is minor. Finding the best move can be a waste of time.

Masters excel in recognizing when the difference between best and second-best is major:

Adams – Pert

Hastings 2021

White to move

Black threatens 30...♜e8+ and then 31 ♔f2 ♗e3+.

When White studied the position he appreciated that he had a wide choice. The alternatives varied widely in quality.

For example, 30 ♕e5? would lose to 30...♜d8!. Also bad was 30 ♕d7 ♕e4+ (31 ♔f2 ♗e3+ 32 ♔e1 ♕f3).

It turned out that only **30 ♔f2!** was good. It was worth finding the best move.

Then it was Black's turn to sift through a broad choice.

Black to move

Three of his candidate moves – 30...♛c6, 30...g6 and 30...f5 – would leave White with the better winning chances.

But none was clearly the best move. It didn't pay for Black to try to find one.

However, he played **30...♛h2+??**.

Again White had only one good move and it did pay to find it. Black resigned soon after **31 ♗g2** because his queen would be trapped following 32 ♖h1!.

45. *What did you mean by a candidate move?*

A candidate move is one that stands out because it does something useful, such as making a threat or defending against one.

A standard way of choosing a move is to identify all the candidate moves and then analyze them one by one.

Gormally – Turner

Hastings 2021

White to move

There are several moves that fit the candidate move description.

For example, 17 ♛d2 and 17 ♛d3 develop White's last undeveloped piece. Advancing a piece, 17 ♘e5, also makes some sense. Even 17 ♗b1, with the idea of preparing ♛d3 and ♛xh7 mate, is worth considering.

A master would start by analyzing the forcing moves. That led White to look at **17 d5!** and its consequences, **17...exd5 18 ♗xd5**.

46. *What is a forcing move?*

A forcing move severely limits the replies by the opponent.

If it had been Black's turn to move in the previous diagram, he could choose among several candidate moves, such as 17...♛d7.

But he didn't have that liberty because **17 d5!** forced him to meet the threat of 18 dxc6.

Don't confuse a forcing move with a forced move. If your opponent checks you, it is forcing. If you have only one legal reply, it is forced.

Masters use this term in a broader sense to mean the only good move. In the last example, 17...exd5 was not forced because Black had a valid alternative in 17...♗xc3.

Most of the moves in a typical game are neither forcing nor forced. In the last example, play went **17...exd5 18 ♗xd5 ♗xc3 19 ♖xc3**.

Gormally – Turner

Hastings 2021

Black to move

Then it was Black's turn to choose among candidate moves. He picked **19...♘a5**. And after **20 ♖xc8 ♕xc8** White had a broad choice.

He soon won, thanks to a blunder, **21 ♘e5 ♗xd5 22 ♕xd5 ♕a8?** and then **23 ♕d7 ♕b7 24 b4! resigns**.

47. *What are the most common kinds of forcing moves?*

A check or a threat to win material. They demand the most respect.

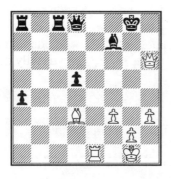

Carlsen – Firouzja

Wijk aan Zee 2021

Black to move

White has just played his queen to h6. It is forcing because it threatens to mate with 38 ♗h7+ ♔h8 39 ♗g6+! ♔g8 40 ♕h7+ ♔f8 41 ♕xf7 mate.

Each of Black's replies was forced. They were the only legal moves.

Black tried to defend against that threat with **37...♕c7**.

Then came **38 ♕h7+ ♔f8 39 ♕h8+ ♗g8 40 ♕h6+.**

Final position

Black resigned because he saw 40...♔f7 41 ♗g6+ ♔f6 42 ♗h5+ ♔f5 43 ♗g4 mate.

Technically, 40...♔f7 was not forced. Even though it was just as bad, Black could have played 40...♕g7 and be mated by 41 ♕d6+! and 42 ♕e7.

Today we know that even in many bad-looking positions there is more than one option.

Aron Nimzovich, a great chess thinker, said that in any solid position there are "at least two alternatives that are the 'only' move."

48. Should I always make a threat if I can?

This works against a weak opponent. He may overlook a tactic and lose.

But when you face stronger opponents, they will spot your threats. A better way to get them to err is to allow them a broader choice of moves.

World Champion Tigran Petrosian was famous for his good, *non-threatening* moves. This gave his opponents wider latitude to make a mistake. "The amazing thing," Bobby Fischer said, "They usually do!"

49. Should I be able to guess my opponent's next move?

Only if the position is fairly simple and if you have plenty of time to think about it – and if you are the world champion.

After Boris Spassky lost his first world championship match, to Petrosian, he encountered another world champion, Mikhail Botvinnik, on a Moscow street. After pleasantries, Botvinnik asked Spassky if he had correctly guessed every one of Petrosian's moves.

No, said Spassky.

"I didn't either," Botvinnik said, referring to the match in which he lost his championship title to Petrosian.

Spassky understood: He should try to guess better the next time. He did. Even though some of Petrosian's moves surprised him in their second match, Spassky won and became world champion.

50. How can I guess if my opponent has so many possible moves?

You can't guess correctly all the time. But you should look for the move by your opponent that is objectively his best.

If he plays an inferior move, you've lost nothing. Here is a striking example of an incorrect guess.

Svidler – Topalov

Elista 1998

Black to move

Black played **17...♛f3**. He was certain 18 ♛xf3 was the best reply.

So, when White chose **18 ♛d2** instead, Black continued as if he had guessed right. He played 18...♞xf3 – capturing his own queen.

After he realized his error, he played **18...♛c6.** There was no damage except to his pride. White's move was inferior and Black quickly won.

José Capablanca said the better you are at guessing your opponent's next move, the stronger you become.

But do not expect to guess even half of your opponent's moves. There are just too many possibilities and most will be "quiet" moves.

51. Do masters analyze every candidate move?

Not at all. Their thinking is often based on general impressions, gut feelings and other personal factors.

Garry Kasparov explained what was going on in his mind at a pivotal moment in his online game against "the World."

Kasparov – "The World"

Internet 1999

White to move

Kasparov's opponents, scattered across the globe, voted for each Black move. The majority had just selected 18...f5.

Kasparov came to basic conclusions: First, he recognized that a trade of queens would favor Black's extra pawns in an endgame.

His team of helpers wanted to investigate 19 ♕xb6. "But I didn't even consider it," he said. "It went against my chess principles." (He was right because Black would stand splendidly after 19 ♕xb6? ♘d4!.)

He made his decision based on a general concept: "It is vital for me to generate attacking chances against the king at d7." This led him to the best move, **19 ♗g5!**.

He said he didn't see all the consequences. "It was just an intuitive decision. It had to be right." (He won after a double-edged endgame.)

52. What if I can't see any good moves to play?

This means your position is difficult. If it is lost, there is little you can do.

But if not, there are two ways to handle it.

One is to broaden your search. If you can't find a move that is good, make sure the alternatives are bad.

This allows you to use the process of elimination.

Hellers – Khalifman

New York 1990

Black to move

This was the crucial game in the last round of a big-bucks tournament. White threatens 19 ♗f4 and ♘g6.

Black found fault with several of his options. He saw that 18...♕xe5? would lose to 19 ♖d8+! ♔xd8 20 ♗xb6+ and ♕xe5.

He also saw that 18...♗d6 19 ♖xd6! and 18...♗b4, 19 ♘d3! would turn out badly.

What remains was the unlikely **18...♖g8!**.

Then 19 ♗f4? ♘bd7 is bad for White after 20 ♘g6? ♕a5!.

Black's position gradually got better, and he won the game and the $20,000 first prize.

53. *What is the other option when you can't find a good move?*

Pass. You can't actually refuse to move, but you can play something that changes the position very little.

Fabiano Caruana was a world class player when he described his thinking in a key game: He recognized he had no constructive move. But he also saw his opponent did not have one either. "I decided to give the move to my opponent," he said.

He made a quiet move. His opponent replied with his own quiet move. After a few more moves of little consequence, Caruana found a way to launch what turned out to be one of his greatest attacks.

"Every move should have a purpose" – but in some cases, the purpose can simply be to stop the position from confusing you.

54. *What should I do when it's my opponent's turn to move?*

First, relax and collect your thoughts.

Consider the position in general terms. Ask yourself questions such as "How could I lose the game quickly?" and "What is his weakest point?" Or think about a potential endgame. "Who stands better if the queens were off the board?"

Another way to collect your thoughts is to explain the position to an imaginary spectator. For example, you might tell this spectator:

"I think I have the advantage. The reason is my bishops are stronger than his. And my knight is well placed. I don't see how he can threaten my king or do any damage to me in the next few moves. If we trade queens, the endgame should be at least equal." And so on.

34

55. When would I be justified in playing a strange-looking move?

It takes experience to understand the difference between "strange" and "bad." But one justification is when your opponent violates general principles first.

An example is a standard opening that begins **1 b3 e5 2 ♗b2 ♘c6 3 e3 ♘f6 4 ♗b5.**

White has violated a rule, "Knights before bishops," in order to threaten to win a pawn with 5 ♗xc6 and 6 ♗xe5.

This entitles Black to consider blocking the d-pawn with **4...♗d6.**

Then comes **5 ♘a3.**

Black to move

This is another odd move that makes a threat, 6 ♘c4 followed by ♘xd6+.

The best reply is the equally odd **5...♘a5!**.

If White can put a knight on the edge of the board, so can Black. Chances are roughly equal after 6 ♘c4 ♘xc4.

56. What is the best advice when it is your turn to move?

It is also the oldest chess advice: In the 10th century a master named Al-Lajlaj said, "When you see a good move, look for a better one."

57. Final question: When should I resign?

When you are absolutely certain that you are lost – and your opponent knows how to win. Not before.

Pachman – Lundin

Leipzig 1960

Black to move

This was played in the days of adjourned games. The first playing session ended with Black sealing his next move in an envelope, to be opened when play resumed.

After analyzing this position for most of the night, White went to the tournament ready to resign. He could not see how to stop the Black kingside pawns from advancing.

Before he could concede, Black resigned – because he had sealed **41...f3??**, allowing mate after 42 ♖c8! and ♖h8.

Your opponent may be annoyed when you play out a lost position. But there is no other penalty.

Choosing a move becomes harder, not easier, as you learn more about chess. You discover there are many factors to consider in evaluating your next step. The most important is what we'll tackle next – tactics.

Chapter Four: Tactics

58. *What exactly are tactics?*

Tactics are the short-term exploitation of your opponent's pieces. The typical goal is to win material, anything from a pawn to a queen.

Most tactics are based on attacking two things at once. In essence, a tactic wins because your opponent cannot make two moves in a row to meet both of your threats.

59. *Can you win a game without tactics?*

Yes, but victory usually occurs because someone resigns before a decisive tactic. A player can justifiably give up before a single capture is made.

Nuber – Keckeisen

Mengen 1994

1 e4 b6 2 d4 e6 3 &d3 &b7 4 ♘f3 g6 5 0-0 &g7 6 ♘bd2 ♘e7 7 ♖e1 0-0 8 ♘f1 d6 9 ♕e2 ♘d7 10 &g5 ♕e8 11 ♖ad1 a5 12 c3 ♖c8 13 ♘g3 ♔h8 14 ♕d2 ♘g8 15 h3 e5 16 &c2 h6 17 &e3 ♖d8 18 ♘h2 ♔h7 19 f4 f6 20 ♕f2 ♘e7 21 ♖d2 ♖h8 22 f5 g5 23 &d1 ♖b8 24 &h5 ♕f8 25 ♘g4 &a6 26 ♖ed1 b5 27 b4 a4 28 a3 &b7 29 ♖d3 ♘c6?? 30 &g6+ ♔g8 31 ♕a2+

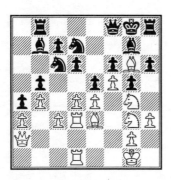

Black to move

The position had been so blockaded that tactics were not possible.

But this changed when White made a disguised threat at move 29, and Black overlooked it.

Black resigned one move before 31...♕f7 32 ♕xf7 mate.

37

60. Do tactics occur most often in the middlegame?

Most do. But you will find many opportunities in the opening. So will your opponent.

The reason is that double attacks exploit unguarded pieces. The time when pieces are most often unprotected is in the first ten moves.

Pambalos – Shavtvaladze

Thessaloniki 2004

1 e4 g6 2 d4 ♗g7 3 ♘c3 c6 4 ♘f3 d5 5 ♗f4 dxe4 6 ♘xe4 ♕a5+

White to move

Both 7 ♕d2 and 7 ♗d2 are good moves. But after **7 c3?? ♕f5!** White lost a piece.

Endgames also have quite a number of tactical opportunities.

61. Why? Aren't there fewer pieces then?

Yes, and that makes it more likely that pieces will be unprotected.

Tactics lurk below the surface of most endgames.

Carlsen – Nakamura

Internet 2020

Black to move

In a drawable endgame, Black erred with **50...♝d5??**.

White answered with the pinning **51 ♖d7!**.

This either wins material (51...♝xe4? 52 ♖xd2) or gains time to queen the a-pawn.

Black resigned after **51...♚e6 52 ♖d8!** maintained the pin and then **52...c4 53 a6 c3 54 ♖xd5**.

One way for improving players to sharpen their tactical skill is to try to solve composed studies, of the "White to play and win" type.

They are always tactical. They end with checkmate or the win of a decisive amount of material.

62. Do I have to know the names for all the different tactics – skewer and x-ray attack and decoy and so on?

The names help you recognize them when they are available. But don't worry about this.

Some tactics have more than one name. For example, "deflection" is called "overloading" as well as "exploiting an overworked piece." All you need to know is how it works.

So – Dubov

Internet 2020

White to move

What they mean is a defensive piece is attacked in a way that it has to relinquish protection of another piece.

Here **31 ♖e8!** prepared to overload the defense of Black's first rank with 32 ♕a8! or the prettier 32 ♕d7!.

Then came **31...♝a7 32 ♕d7!** based on 32...♕xd7 33 ♝xf6+.

Black resigned after **32...h6 33 ♕c8! ♖xe8 34 ♕xe8+ ♚h7:**

39

White to move

And now **35 ♗xf6!** deflected the queen from a mating square (35...♕xf6 36 ♕g8 mate or 35...♕g6 36 ♕h8 mate).

63. What other useful terms should I know?

You can start with discovered check.

It is a bit misleading for beginners. They may believe it means both players suddenly discover one of them was in check. "Uncovered" check describes it better.

This tactic is important to learn early in your chess career because it helps explain a hierarchy of checks:

Discovered checks are typically stronger than a normal check. And double check is often a fortified discovered check. Essentially it means a discovered check in which the moving piece also delivers check.

64. So double check is always stronger?

Often, not always.

Dubov – Anton Guijarro

Internet 2020

White to move

White would be better after the double checking 42 ♖xe7+.

But much stronger is **42 ♖e4+!** so that 42...♔f8 43 ♕b4 creates a fatal pin.

40

Black resigned after **42…♚e8 43 ♕g8+ ♚d7 44 ♖d4+** in view of 42…♚c7 43 ♕d8+ and ♕xe7 or 42…♚c6 43 ♕d5+ and ♕d6+.

65. What other tactical terms are easy to understand?

Fork. It simply means one piece simultaneously attacks two enemy pieces.

The forking piece is most often a queen, a knight or a pawn.

Rooks and bishops can also fork but their primary tactic is something that a knight and a pawn cannot do. They can pin.

66. How exactly is pin defined?

Like many technical chess terms, a diagram explains it better than words.

Aronian – Ding Liren

Internet 2021

White to move

Black is lost because **33 ♕e8!** sets up a decisive pin, 34 ♖d7!.

The Black queen could not then leave the second rank because that would illegally expose his king to check.

Black can avoid the pin but would have to make a decisive concession (33…♕xc3 34 ♖d7+, for example). He resigned instead.

Some Web sites talk about an "absolute pin" and a "relative pin." And "absolute" means a pin cannot be legally broken because if the pinned piece moved it would expose the king to check, as in this example. But these are textbook words, not used in everyday chess talk.

67. Is winning material the only reason to make a pin?

You will beat a lot of fellow novices with a material-winning pin. But better opponents won't allow that to happen to them.

However, you might use pins against them to gain time.

68. *What does time have to do with it?*

A pin can just be an inconvenience. The pinned piece may be able to free itself after a few un-pinning moves.

Black to move

This is a popular opening position. The White bishop's pin of the f6-knight is annoying but does not win material by force.

Black can break the pin with pawn moves, 8...h6 9 ♗h4 g5.

But then 10 ♘xg5! hxg5 11 ♗xg5 reestablishes the pin with a powerful plan of 12 f4!. This threatens to win with fxe5 and the fork ♗xf6.

The best unpinning method, believe it or not, is **8...♕e7** followed by ...♘d8-e6.

For example, **9 ♖e1 ♘d8 10 d4 ♘e6 11 ♗h4 ♘f4**.

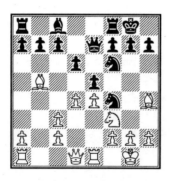

White to move

It may take two further moves to break the pin. But White cannot exploit the situation and the position would be roughly equal after **12 ♗f1 ♘g6 13 ♗g5 h6!**, for example.

42

69. *Should I always pin when I can?*

"Inflict a pin, as a general rule, whenever possible," wrote former World Champion Max Euwe. But he was writing for novices.

If it does not win material, a pinning piece can be misplaced. For example, a popular opening begins **1 e4 e5 2 ♘f3 ♘c6 3 ♗b5 a6 4 ♗a4 ♘f6 5 0-0 ♗e7 6 ♖e1 b5 7 ♗b3 d6 8 c3**.

Black to move

Now 8...♗g4 tries to discourage 9 d4 because 9...0-0 10 h3? ♗xf3! 11 ♕xf3 loses a pawn to 11...exd4.

But 9 h3 ♗h5 10 d3! leads to a good position for White because Black's bishop is out of play.

White will play ♘bd2-f1-g3 and then ♘xh5, if allowed.

Better in the diagram is 8...0-0, waiting for 9 d4 ♗g4!. White usually avoids the pin with 9 h3! and then 10 d4.

70. *What else do tactical moves do besides attack and restrict?*

They can act as a screen to shield another piece.

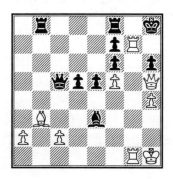

Papaioannou – Kveinys

Plovdiv 2003

White to move

With **32 ☖1g5!** the rook serves as a screen.

It cuts the Black bishop's protection of h6 (32...fxg5 3 ♕xh6 mate).

Black resigned in view of 32...♗xg5 33 hxg5 ♔xg7 34 ♕xh6+ and mate after 35 gxf6.

71. Are there rarer tactics that are worth knowing?

Yes, one of them is a zwischenzug. It is easiest to understand as an in-between-move. It can improve a forcing sequence by being inserted between two moves.

Miles – Timman

Amsterdam 1985

White to move

After **18 ♕d5+!** the forced reply is **18...♕xd5**.

Then, instead of 19 cxd5, White inserts 19 ♘xe7+! and ♘xd5.

You can say the winning tactic was a fork (**19 ♘xe7+**) but it is also a zwischenzug.

Zwischenzugs are tricky because when you upset the normal sequence of moves, your opponent might be able to insert his own zwischenzug.

72. How does that happen?

An example is an opening trap that begins **1 e4 c5 2 c3 d5 3 exd5 ♕xd5 4 d4 ♘c6 5 ♘f3 ♗g4 6 ♘bd2 ♘f6 7 ♗c4 ♗xf3**.

White to move

Now 8 ♕xf3 ♕xf3 is fine for Black. And not 8 ♘xf3?? ♕xc4.

White has a zwischenzug, **8 ♕a4**.

Black's queen is attacked and he would be a bit worse after 8...♕d7 9 ♘xf3. If that happens, the zwischenzug will have succeeded.

But Black has a trick of his own, **8...♗d1!**.

Then he is better after 9 ♗xd5 ♗xa4 but also after 9 ♔xd1 ♕xg2 or 9 ♕xd1 ♕xg2.

This brings up another term. The Black bishop could be called a desperado.

73. And what is that?

A desperado is a desperate piece. It tries to inflict as much damage as it can before it is captured. A case of dueling desperados:

Bogolyubov – Schmid
Bad Pyrmont 1949

1 e4 e5 2 ♘f3 ♘c6 3 ♘c3 ♘f6 4 d4 exd4 5 ♘xd4 ♘xe4

Black's move is based on a pin, 6 ♘xe4 ♕e7!. Then Black regains his knight (7 ♕e2?? ♘xd4).

White's best reply is **6 ♘xc6!** so that 6...dxc6?? 7 ♘xe4 wins a piece.

Black to move

Black's knight became a desperado when it played **6...♘xc3!**

Black would be a pawn ahead after the routine 7 bxc3 dxc6.

Therefore, White replied **7 ♘xd8!**.

The two doomed knights wanted to inflict maximum damage before they were captured, **7...♘xd1 8 ♘xf7 ♘xf2 9 ♘xh8 ♘xh1**.

If either player had stopped, he would have ended up behind in material (e.g. 8 ♔xd1? ♔xd8).

The irony is that they were still on the board 16 moves later when the game ended:

10 ♗d3 ♝c5 11 ♗xh7 ♞f2 12 ♗f4 d6 13 ♗g6+ ♚f8 14 ♗g3 ♞g4 15 ♞f7 ♞e3 16 ♚d2 ♝f5 17 ♞g5 ♝xg6 18 ♞e6+ ♚e7 19 ♞xc5 ♞xc2 20 ♗h4+ ♚e8 21 ♞e6 ♚d7 22 ♞f4 ♞xa1 23 ♞xg6 ♖e8 24 ♗f2 ♞c2 25 ♞f4 ♞b4 26 resigns.

White resigned because the tactics are over, the smoke has cleared and he is the Exchange and a pawn down.

There are many tactical finesses to learn. Fortunately, there are also many good resources for the curious student.

Several good Web sites and books have quiz positions with the task "White to play and win" or "Black to play and win." The solutions are typically two or three moves long. Even grandmasters try to solve these quizzes on a regular basis, to keep in tactical shape.

Tactics play the central role in almost every game played below the master level. They generate threats and typically pose the greatest problems for your opponents. Until you meet stronger players, many of your games will be decided when you or your opponent make a tactical mistake.

Chapter Five: Mistakes

74. Why do players make so many mistakes?

Because there are many more ways to go wrong in chess than in any other game.

In a typical position, only about 10 percent of the legal moves are good moves. Most of the others are mediocre.

But at least 10 percent are downright bad. In other words, there are as many bad moves as good ones.

As Savielly Tartakower put it, "The mistakes are there, waiting to be made."

75. In my games, mistakes turn out to be more important than good moves. Is that normal?

Absolutely. Most games played below the master level are decided by mistakes.

That is good news:

Most of your victories will come by exploiting your opponent's errors. You don't have to be a middlegame genius or endgame wizard to win.

76. But masters must make more good moves than mistakes, don't they?

Yes, but even in master games the errors can come quickly.

The evidence is vivid, literally, on the Web site Chessbomb.com. It conducts real-time coverage of major events. When a player makes a bad move it appears in a shade of red.

In the first major tournament of 2021, games with plenty of bright red moves appeared:

Duda – Nepomniachtchi

Internet 2021

White to move

White would have winning pressure after the pinning 54 ♕b4!.

Yet he played **54 ♕d3??**.

Black overlooked the pinning 54...♖a3! and replied **54...♕b6?**.

Then came **55 ♔f4? ♖a2 56 g4? ♕b2**.

White might draw after 57 ♖xe7+ ♔xe7 58 ♔g5.

But he chose **57 ♕d1??**.

Black to move

Black has a simple win, 57...♕h2+ 58 ♔e3 ♖a3+.

However, the game ended with **57...♔e6?? 58 ♕h1?? ♕d2+ 59 ♔g3 ♕f2+**.

White resigned in view of mate next move (60 ♔f4 g5 or 60 ♔h3 ♕h4).

And this is far from unique in a grandmaster game played at a quick speed.

77. Why do good players make bad mistakes?

The primary causes are a lapse in concentration or a miscalculation.

There are underlying reasons and they apply to all players: Mistakes happen due to tiredness, shortness of time, overconfidence, greed, indecisiveness or feeling under pressure.

78. I see the terms "blunder," "decisive error," "oversight," "inaccuracy" and others. What are the differences?

A blunder usually means a major error, such as allowing mate or the loss of a significant amount of material.

An inaccuracy typically describes a second-best move, a minor error.

An oversight may be overlooking or underestimating an opponent's reply. It may be a major or minor mistake, depending on how strong the reply.

There are two types of errors that get labeled "decisive." One is a move responsible for losing a relatively safe position. The other is a minor mistake that is the last error in a series and renders a very bad position untenable.

Artemiev – Matlakov

Moscow 2020

Black to move

A balanced position became bad for Black after **38...g5?**.

He overlooked how **39 ♗d5!** would threaten 40 ♖xf7! ♖xf7 41 ♖e8+.

He might have resisted with 39...♖xd3 but played **39...gxh4?**.

Then **40 ♖xf7! ♖xf7?** allowed White to end matters with **41 ♖e8+ ♔h7 42 ♕h5+ ♕h6 43 ♕xf7**.

Black made three bad moves in a row. But the middle one, 39...gxh4?, was considered decisive because Black's position could not be saved after it.

These terms can be confusing because a master will use them in whatever way he wants. He will say he "blundered" a pawn. Or that a minor error was a "positional blunder."

79. *Do masters make the same kind of mistakes as I do?*

Masters make very few simple tactical errors. They also avoid mistakes due to inexperience and lack of knowledge.

A mistake stemming from a lack of knowledge is falling into an opening trap, losing an easily drawable endgame or failing to recognize a tactical pattern.

80. *What do you mean by a tactical pattern?*

Many winning tactics occur in similar positions. What makes it a recognizable pattern is just a few pieces and pawns.

If a pattern is slightly different, even a world champion can fail to recognize it and blunder.

Deep Fritz – Kramnik

Bonn 2006

Black to move

The position would be roughly equal after 34...♔g8.

Without much thought, Black – the reigning world champion – chose **34...♕e3??**.

He was surprised by **35 ♕h7 mate**.

Masters who witnessed this blamed it on the unusual kingside position.

If the White knight were on g5 and Black had just played ...h6, then the ♕h7 mate pattern would be a familiar one. Kramnik would have seen it.

This also illustrates an irony of chess knowledge. The more you know, the more confident you become. This is good.

But it may make you careless. You can move quickly in positions that you would have taken more time to ponder when you knew less.

81. What kind of opponent's moves are players most likely to overlook?

We train ourselves to look for forcing, tactical moves and moves based on general principles, such as advancing a piece.

This makes us vulnerable to overlooking a retreat of a well-placed piece.

Here is one that slipped past Bobby Fischer's tactical radar.

Fischer – Burger

San Francisco 1964

1 e4 e5 2 ♘f3 ♘c6 3 ♗c4 ♘f6 4 ♘g5 d5 5 exd5 ♘d4 6 c3 b5 7 ♗f1 ♘xd5 8 cxd4 ♕xg5 9 ♗xb5+ ♔d8 10 ♕f3 ♗b7 11 0-0 exd4 12 ♕xf7??

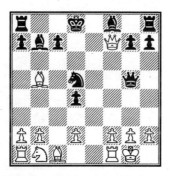

Black to move

In this game from a simultaneous exhibition, Bobby resigned after Black played **12...♘f6!**.

It stops both of the threatened mates (♕d7 and ♕e8).

But it also threatens to win the bishop (...♕xb5) as well as deliver mate (...♕xg2).

82. I make a lot of mistakes. How long would I last against a grandmaster?

Here's another irony: If you make a minor error very early in a game you might last much longer than if you blundered later.

For example, if you lost a pawn in the first 10 moves, the grandmaster would know that he could win in the most secure way. He could gradually trade pieces and beat you in an endgame.

The game would last twice as long as if you blundered away a piece on Move 20.

83. When I play over a master game it always seems that mistakes are immediately punished. Is that common?

No, many mistakes go unnoticed by both players. And others are not punished because of a counter-error.

Karpov – Sveshnikov

Riga 2015

Black to move

Black played **32...♖d2??** and allowed 33 ♖a8+! and 34 ♖d8. This would pin the bishop and win material.

But White played a natural positional move, **33 ♘c5??**. The Russians call this phenomenon an "exchange of kindnesses."

Tartakower said the winner of a game is the player "who makes the next to last mistake." He was right in this case. Black escaped the pin. But he made a critical error on move 38. Because there were no more mistakes, he lost.

84. Those moves got an "??" and, in other games, a mistake is given an "?". What is the difference?

A move has to be pretty bad to be assigned a double-question-mark. But there is wide variation in the awarding of a single question mark.

Some annotators consider "?" appropriate for a minor error, such as damaging your pawn structure. Others say only a more serious error, such as any loss of material, deserves a question mark.

Don't pay too much attention to the punctuation. The question marks are there so you'll appreciate how the game takes its course.

85. How many mistakes does it take to lose a game played by opponents of equal strength?

Usually it is one big error or three or four minor ones.

After a minor mistake, the position becomes harder to play. It is more difficult to find good moves and easier to make really bad ones. Even a quite unintentional move, like a "fingerfehler," can become more likely.

86. What is a fingerfehler?

You could call it a digital error, in the sense that your fingers are digits.

It happens when you touch the wrong piece and have to move it. Or you pick up the piece you wanted but put it on the wrong square and let go.

Alexander Alekhine began a game with **1 e4 e6 2 d4 d5 3 ♘c3 ♗b4**. He intended to continue 4 e5 and, if 4...c5, then 5 ♗d2.

But he got the order of moves wrong and played **4 ♗d2**.

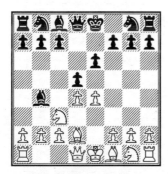

Black to move

Black won a pawn, **4...dxe4 5 ♘xe4 ♕xd4!**.

White, nevertheless, won the game and the opening has become known as the "Fingerslip Variation."

Today there's a more common digital mistake, a mouseslip.

87. And that is?

What it sounds like: You are playing on-line and your cursor moves a piece to the wrong square.

Nepomniachtchi – Carlsen

Internet 2020

Black to move

Magnus Carlsen's position is nearly a forced win. He had to choose a retreat for his queen, such as to b5, b6 or b7.

He moved it but it stopped short, **38...♕b4??**, due to a mouseslip. He resigned immediately.

88. You mentioned something called a positional blunder. What is that?

It is a mistake that makes a significant concession but the consequences are neither immediate nor costly in terms of material.

Faulty pawn moves are the most common positional blunders. Here's a version.

Tarrasch – Michel

Semmering 1926

Black to move

White has just captured on d5. He would have some positional advantage after 22...exd5 because his entrenched knight is superior to the Black bishop.

Black retook **22...cxd5** so that his bishop would have more scope on queenside squares.

But 22...cxd5? made White's c5-pawn a potential passed pawn. Without making another major error he was ground down:

23 b4 ♖d8 24 ♖c1 bxc5 25 bxc5 ♕a5 26 ♕c3 ♕xc3 27 ♖xc3 ♖c7
28 ♖b3 ♗c6 29 f4! ♞f8 30 ♖eb1 ♔e7 31 ♔f2 h5 32 ♖b8 ♖cd7 33 ♔g3
f6 34 ♖c8 ♖xc8 35 ♞xc8+ ♔f7 36 ♖b3 ♖c7 37 ♞d6+ ♔g6 38 ♖e3 ♗d7
39 f5+ exf5 40 ♖e7 f4+ 41 ♔xf4 resigns.

Most amateurs are not punished for their positional errors.

89. Why not?

Because their opponents aren't good enough to punish them.

Until you are an average-strength player, your tactical mistakes will be
the ones that cost you more often.

When you improve, you are more likely to be punished for other errors
such as oversights based on faulty assumption.

90. What do you mean by assumption?

This is an essential element in calculation. You make a move based on
an assumption of how your opponent will reply.

You can't calculate without some expectation like that. If your
assumption is invalid, the calculation fails.

Peralta – Zysk

Athens 2006

Black to move

Black's knight is pinned (11...♞f7 12 ♗xg7).

But he thought he could not only escape but win material with **11...♞f3+**
and 12...♗xb2.

What he assumed was White would capture with a piece on f3.

What he overlooked was **12 exf3!** so that 12...♗xb2 13 ♕e2+! regains
the bishop, at a piece profit.

91. I've read masters saying they suffered an "hallucination." What is that?

A kind of blind spot. You foresee a future move without realizing it cannot legally happen.

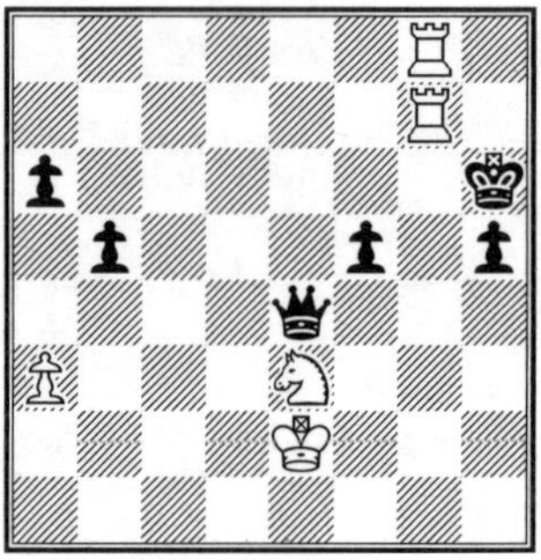

Caruana – Dominguez

St. Louis 2018

White to move

White should win gradually, beginning with 54 ♖g1 and the threat of 55 ♖h8 mate.

He played **54 ♖e7??.** He visualized 54…♕xe7 55 ♘xf5+ and ♘xe7.

But when he saw that 55 ♘xf5+ was illegal he resigned.

There are several versions of this kind of error. These are tricks your mind plays on you, such as a retained image.

92. What is that?

It is when you think that certain characteristics of the position in front of you will remain true after a series of moves.

You retain the image that turns out to be false.

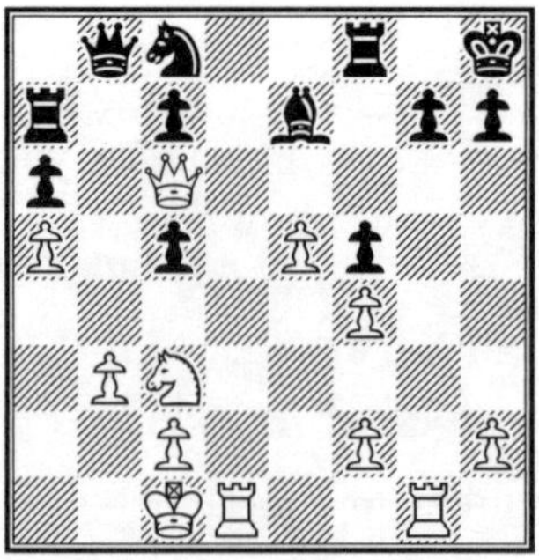

Benko – Kavalek

Wijk aan Zee 1969

White to move

White saw an apparently winning sacrifice, **21 ♖xg7**.

It was based on **21…♔xg7 22 ♖g1+ ♔h8 23 ♕g2** "and mates."

What he overlooked is that Black can protect g7 by means of **23...♗f6!** (24 exf6 c6!). Black went on to win.

The key defensive move, ...c6, was not possible in the diagram. White retained that image.

93. *I see how masters blunder when they are short of time. Do they ever blunder when they relax?*

Yes. After a time control has been reached, it is natural to calm down – and become careless.

Anand – Adams

London 2014

White to move

The time control had just ended. Without calculating much, White played **41 ♗c4** because a trade of bishops would seem to benefit him.

But this loses to **41...♕d1!** with 42...♖a1 and ...♕h1 mate to come.

White resigned after **42 ♕h6 ♗h3+!** because he was getting mated.

That illustrates the best way to detect a blunder.

94. *What is that?*

Look carefully at your opponent's last move.

You should first examine it to see if it makes a threat that you must respond to. But you should also ask "What did this allow?"

If it is a blunder, the answer will tell you.

95. *How do I get my opponent to err?*

If we only knew that, we would all be challenging the world champion in a match.

The natural way is to set traps or make threats, if possible on every move. This may work against opponents who can't detect a threat.

But as you improve as a player, you will face more experienced opponents. They will be able to see your threats and defend against them, as noted in the answer to Question 48.

To get better than that you need to learn how to place your opponent under continuous pressure. Magnus Carlsen explained grandmaster errors when he said, "When you put pressure on your opponent they tend to make mistakes."

96. What does pressure mean?

It often means to restrict an opponent's pieces and be able to threaten his material when you are ready. An opponent under pressure may have a choice of reasonable-looking moves but some of them are errors.

Carlsen – Georgiadis

Biel 2018

White to move

White had pressed Black but the likely outcome now is a draw. White tried to keep the pressure on with 46 a4.

It gives Black the idea of winning with **46...b3** and 47...♗a3!. There is only one defense but it wins: **46 ♘f3!** resigns because of ♘d2xc4!.

97. Why does it seem there are more mistakes in endgames?

Part of that is an illusion. Part is true.

The illusion comes because we can spot mistakes more easily in endgames. Databases reveal the absolutely best moves in certain positions with few pieces and pawns.

But there are also more blunders in endings. The reason is fatigue.

The longer a player presses his opponent, the more likely the opponent will err. Ask any of the dozen-plus grandmasters who lost a game to Carlsen that lasted 90 moves or more.

Databases say the longest decisive game of 2019 was this:

Shkuratov – Gubajdallin

St. Petersburg 2019

White to move

(The position has not changed substantially in the last 125 moves!).

The only change in that time is that Black advanced his two pawns and won a pawn.

White could continue to defend with 163 ♖e3+ and shift his took to protected squares such as f3.

Instead, he chose **163 ♖c3??** and resigned after **163...♛b6+! 164 ♔e1 ♛a5 165 ♔d2 ♔d4** because his rook is lost. Or 164 ♔f1 ♛f6+!.

98. How do I reduce the number of my own blunders?

A good first step is diagnostic. Conduct an *error profile* of yourself.

Go through your lost games. It's painful but revealing. Identify the worst mistakes and/or the final mistake with a computer:

How many were gross blunders? (For example, you left a piece en prise and it was captured.)

How many were oversights? (You completely overlooked your opponent's powerful move.)

How many allowed simple tactics? (You allowed the pin that won your queen.)

How many were positional mistakes? (You traded your best piece and ruined your pawn structure.)

What was the status of the game? (You were winning, better, equal, worse, lost.)

When did the error occur? (Opening, middlegame or endgame.)

This will give you a profile that reveals to which type of error you are prone. It won't stop you from repeating them but it may provide you with warning signs that read "Blunder Ahead."

Chapter Six: Studying

99. Why is learning chess so hard?

Because there is so much to know before you can even play badly.

Fortunately, the hardest part is at the very beginning. It gets easier after that.

100. What is the best way to study chess?

There is no best way for everyone. But there is one helpful guideline: Studying should be enjoyable.

If you don't like what you are doing – such as trying to memorize different rook-and-pawn endgame positions – you will give up studying endgames. Or give up chess.

101. Do I need some kind of study plan or schedule?

It isn't necessary if you regularly feed your interest in chess in your own way.

Magnus Carlsen never had a study schedule he enjoyed. "My first trainer would sometimes give me some homework that I wouldn't really like," he recalled. "Sometimes I'd do it, sometimes I wouldn't."

"But then instead I might have thought about some chess problems in my head or read a chess book or just moved the pieces around a bit on my own. And I think it was just as useful training in the long run."

102. How can something that casual be useful?

Just examining a position you see on the Internet or in a book or magazine can be instructive if you make proper use of it.

Try to figure out what you would do if it were your position and your move. This prompts you to think critically.

In the following position ou can start by asking yourself basic questions:

What is the material situation? You can figure out quickly that Black is a pawn ahead.

Wojtazsek – Caruana

Wijk aan Zee 2021

Black to move

What is White threatening? Nothing.

Since Black has a broad choice you can ask more questions: How does he make progress? Which of his pieces can he put on better squares? How can Black open the position favorably?

This is a difficult position and you may not find the best plan. (It is opening the e-file for his rooks.)

Or you may see that plan but have trouble figuring out how to do it. (With ...♘f4 and ...c6/...d5 is best.)

But you will be following one of the most important principles of studying: Every diagram you encounter should be a lesson.

"Any analysis you do is good," as Grandmaster Yasser Seirawan said.

103. I click through games all the time on the Internet. How often should I stop and try to analyze?

The best times are usually the most puzzling times. They are the positions when you wonder, "What would I do here?"

The game we were just looking at continued **28...♘f4! 29 ♗f1 c6! 30 ♕f2 ♖e6 31 ♖c3 d5! 32 g3 hxg3 33 hxg3 dxe4 34 gxf4? gxf4+ 35 ♕g2**.

Black to move

Some of those moves will be mysterious to you. Don't be surprised. That is going to happen often when you examine a grandmaster game.

This is a good time to stop because it looks like Black should have a strong, perhaps decisive move. How many moves would you consider playing? Don't calculate them yet. Just figure out which could be considered candidate moves.

After thinking about it for a few minutes, you might conclude that both of the captures on f3 are worth a deeper look.

If you take some more time, you might see that 35...e3 would also prepare a capture, 36...♘xf3+.

Once you've done that you can analyze the three candidates. It turns out that 35...♘xf3+ is good but not clearly winning (36 ♖xf3 exf3 37 ♕xg6+).

However, **35...exf3!** works better in view of 36 ♖xf3 ♘xf3+ and wins.

In the game, White resigned after **36 ♕xg6+ ♖xg6+ 37 ♔h1 f2** (also winning is 37...♖g3, with a threat of ...♖e6-h6 mate) **38 ♗h3 ♘c4 39 ♖xc4 ♖e1+ resigns**.

104. How much time should I devote to studying each week?

Quality, not quantity, is what counts.

One hour that leaves you saying "That was interesting!" is worth four hours of "I hate knight endgames but I have to study them today."

One general guideline: Don't study when you are tired. You won't absorb the material well and feel you are wasting your time.

"I want to come to my study period in the same way that you come from the shower, fresh," Seirawan said. He liked to study several hours in a row with that feeling.

105. When I study it is never for more than an hour. Is there hope for me?

If you can do that regularly you are better off than a weekend binge studier. Consistent study reinforces what you've learned.

The first world champion, Wilhelm Steinitz, expressed it in extreme terms: One hour a day for six straight days is better than six hours in one sitting a week, he said.

But even if you only look at chess for one hour every few days you can benefit.

106. Timing aside, what should I be studying?

There are three main topics. The first is you.

Your games. Playing over your past games is the best way to understand how well – and how badly – you can play.

The second topic is master games. Look over the latest Fabiano Caruana win or a collection of José Capablanca games, for examples.

The third is general stuff. Try to solve tactical problems online, check out a new opening in a book, practice calculating two-move variations, and so on.

107. When I look at my games, which ones will teach me the most – my wins or my losses?

You can learn from all of your games. Because they are *your* games, these are the most teachable moments.

You will care more about your moves than about, for example, Hikaru Nakamura's. And you should be able to apply this knowledge to future games.

Bobby Fischer underlined this, after he was lucky to draw an endgame when he was 15.

Gligorić – Fischer

Belgrade 1959

White to move

After **53 ♔xb5?** Fischer played **53...♖b8+ 54 ♔a4 ♖a8+! 55 ♔b3 ♖c8!**.

He was proud that he had seen how he would draw in the resulting pawn endgame, after **56 ♖xc8 ♔xc8 57 ♔c4 ♔b8!**.

He had "won the opposition." We'll get to that in Question 279 but for the time being, you can see how the game could end in stalemate.

That is 58 ♔c5 ♔c7 59 b5 ♔b7 60 b6 ♔b8! 61 ♔c6 ♔c8 62 b7+ ♔b8 63 ♔b6.

It was quickly pointed out to Fischer after the game that he should have lost in the diagram position. White could have played 53 ♖c7+! and then 53...♔d8 54 ♖c5!and ♔xb5.

Fischer didn't believe it was a win:

"I stayed up all night analyzing, finally convincing myself and, incidentally, learning a lot about rook and pawn endings."

What did he learn? He didn't elaborate. But 53...♔d6! would have been a trickier answer to 53 ♖c7+.

However White can still win with 54 ♖c5 and then 54...♖b8+ 55 ♔a7.

There are also finesses to be discovered after 54 ♖c6+ ♔d7 55 ♔xb5.

For example, 55...♖b8+ 56 ♖b6! ♔c7 57 ♖xb8 ♔xb8 58 ♔b6! and this time White wins the opposition and with it the game.

108. *I feel funny finding out how badly I played.*

It helps to know your weaknesses however your learn them. With the help of a computer or a friend, you can find the opportunities you missed.

Ruth Haring, a better than average player, felt embarrassed one day when she came back to her San Francisco home to discover her houseguest had discovered a shoebox filled with scoresheets of her old games. "I was terrified," she recalled – because the houseguest was Bobby Fischer. He was judging her play.

"So, what do you think?" she asked Fischer.

"You're a pretty good player, but you're too pessimistic" he said. She took that as advice and it "helped me with the rest of my life."

This is one of the reasons why honesty is one of the most important traits of a good player.

109. *Can't I just look at my wins?*

You will discover lessons in all of your games, even the ones you thought you played well. You didn't notice your weak moves in a game you won because, well, you won.

But there is a lot of truth in what the writer Fred Reinfeld said: "You can learn much from your losses – although it is infinitely kinder to your ego to learn from someone else's."

To protect your mood – after all, you have to make studying enjoyable – a good study strategy is to look at one of your losses and one of your wins each session.

110. I think I play the opening better than the middlegame. Should I devote more time to what I'm best at?

"Interest is roughly proportional to knowledge," according to Ariel Mengarini, a master and trained psychologist. "You will naturally tend to study deeper that branch of chess which you already know the most about."

The good news: Working on your strengths may get you to a level near that of an average tournament player.

You may, for example, be able to outplay most opponents in the opening. After all, your weakness in the middlegame won't be exposed if you are already a knight ahead by Move 20.

The bad news: As you improve, you will play stronger opponents. They will be just as good as you in the opening – and much better in the middlegame that you neglected to learn.

Mikhail Tal loved tactics all his life and was taught by teachers who loved combinations. But he knew that if he wanted to get better he would need to learn the dull stuff.

Tal – Weldon

Vilnius 1949

White to move

Twelve-year-old Tal finished off with the best moves, **60 ♖f7! ♖h1 61 ♔f8!**.

Black resigned following **61... ♖h8+ 62 ♔g7+ ♖e8 63 ♖f8 ♔d7 64 ♖xe8 ♔xe8 65 ♔f6**.

111. How do grandmasters divide their study time among openings, middlegames and endgames?

They spend the lion's share – as much as 90 percent – on openings. But they can afford to do this because they have already spent gazillions of hours on endgames.

Middlegames, in general, and tactics, in particular, deserve the most of your attention.

Ken Smith, a master and chess book publisher, offered this advice: Until you are at least a better-than-average player, "your first name is 'Tactics,' your middle name is 'Tactics,' and your last name is 'Tactics.'"

Here is an example of what Smith had learned:

Bills – Smith

Houston 1964

Black to move

Smith won with **27...h5! 28 ♕xh5 ♕d6+ 29 ♔f3 ♖f5+ 30 ♔g4 ♖f4+! 31 exf4 ♕xf4 mate.**

112. Is it possible to learn too much of some aspect of chess?

You mean, "If I learn too much about tactics, will I forget how to win an endgame when I'm a rook ahead?"

Of course not. But there is a law of diminishing returns.

As you improve in chess, the role played by tactics in your games will decline somewhat.

Becoming a better tactician then will make you a slightly better player overall. But it won't help you make the same kind of leap in skill that it did when you were a beginner.

113. When I study someone else's game, how long should it take?

Grandmaster Bent Larsen said he spent two hours on each game. You should spend at least that amount because you won't understand the moves as quickly as Larsen did.

If a master took four or five hours to play a game, there was plenty for him to think about.

114. There are an awful lot of games out there. What kind should I study?

Here are some general criteria:

Annotated games are much better than unannotated games.

An annotated game with a lot of words and few long move variations is best.

A computer-annotated game, without words but with evaluations of alternative moves, is better than nothing.

Today's annotators are better than early 20th century writers, who often said nothing more than "Better is 21 ♘c4" and "Also possible is 32 ♖f6."

However, some annotators deliberately avoid explaining simple tactics.

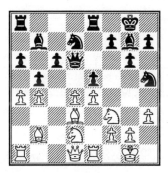

Morozevich – Sasikiran

Biel 2004

White to move

Play went **21 dxe5 ♛xb4** without a comment by White, the annotator.

Readers were bound to wonder: Why couldn't Black win a piece with 21...♛xd3 ?

They had to figure out for themselves that 22 ♖e3! would trap the queen.

115. What other criteria are there for selecting games to study?

You want games that are entertaining. You won't learn much from boring draws.

If you see a game in a book or magazine, look first for the diagrams. This will tell you if the game's key positions are interesting. The annotator usually chooses where to put diagrams and he will probably use them at the key points.

116. When I get through studying a game, what's next?

Look at it again. To get the most out of it, you should examine a game three times.

The first time should be fairly quick, about three minutes if you are using a computer.

You want to get a sense of the flow of the game. Look for moments which could be turning points. When did White's position first seem advantageous? When did it become clear he was winning?

Don't examine the annotations during this first look. That comes during the second time you play over the moves.

Focus on the words, not the variations. Let the annotator explain the principles involved. Let him point out the critical points that you didn't notice the first time you looked at the game.

A good annotator will fill in a lot of gaps. At the end of the second look, you should have a good idea of what the losing player was trying to do and what the winner succeeded in doing.

You might stop there. But it is worth taking one more look. The third time you play through the game is when you should "get into the weeds," the move-analysis. The notes should point out why 37 ♖d2? was the losing move and how White miscalculated.

117. Should I study the games of a particular master?

Yes, hero worship is good.

You might choose a favorite grandmaster who competes regularly. You can find his (or her) latest games on the Internet. This adds a personal involvement in studying.

Or you can choose one of the great players of the past, such as Mikhail Tal or Garry Kasparov.

But your first heroes should be players you can understand, not just emulate. A lot of what happens in Tal or Kasparov games depends on elaborate calculation and deep opening preparation. That can be too confusing.

118. So whose games are appropriate for me?

For beginners, there is no one better than Paul Morphy. You can learn tactics, the use of open lines and the benefits of development in the opening.

When you are ready for the next step, José Capablanca, Siegbert Tarrasch and Vishy Anand will be helpful. They played games based on solid, understandable principles.

Then comes Bobby Fischer, Anatoly Karpov and Magnus Carlsen, among others. Their wins tend to be more complex but also highly instructive.

Saidy – Fischer

New York 1968

Black to move

White has an extra pawn and his more advanced pawns give him an advantage in space. His advantage would be substantial after 12...♗f5 13 g4!.

But with a few surprising moves Fischer restrained White on both wings, **12...h5! 13 a3 a5! 14 b3 ♕g6 15 ♘b2 ♗f5 16 ♕c2**.

He was still a bit worse but managed to create counterplay by getting the most out of his pieces, **16...♘d7! 17 ♖e1 ♘c5 18 ♗f1 ♖a6!** and **...♖b6**. Amid the middlegame complications, he won.

119. I see annotators adding "!?" after a move. What does it mean?

Annotators say it identifies a move that is interesting, surprising, enterprising or just "deserving attention," whatever that means.

But in practice, what the annotator means is "I don't know if this should get an exclamation point or not. But I should say something about it."

120. And what does "?!" mean?

This is slightly less evasive. It usually means "a dubious move." The annotator is not confident enough to award it a question mark.

121. What does it mean when an annotator writes "a won game"?

He means the position can be won with relatively routine moves.

It is similar to saying your material advantage gives you a "technical win" in the endgame. But "a won game" usually means a positional, not a material, advantage.

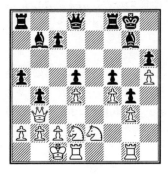

Adams – Topalov

Madrid 1996

White to move

Black said after the game that he was "strategically winning" here. White has no real chances for counterplay because his knights cannot safely reach good squares such as e5.

This did not mean White would lose quickly. "A won game" rarely does. The game went **23 ♖ge1 ♖e8 24 ♘f1 ♗a6 25 ♘g1 ♗c4 26 ♕a4 ♗xf1 27 ♖xf1 ♖e6 28 ♕b3 c6** and Black did not win material until after **29 ♖fe1 ♖xe1 30 ♖xe1 ♗xd4.**

122. But it still takes a lot of calculation to win positions like this, correct?

Not if the position is really "won."

Black did not have to calculate more than two moves ahead since the last diagram. He continued with solid, intuitive moves, **31 ♘e2 ♕e7 32 ♔d1 ♗f2 33 ♖f1 ♗c5 34 ♕d3 ♖e8 35 ♖e1 ♕e6 36 c3 bxc3 37 bxc3.**

Black to move

Black could improve his position further in a variety ways, such as 37...♗b6 and ...c5-c4.

He preferred to calculate and finished off with **37... d4 38 cxd4 ♗b4 39 d5 ♕xd5 40 ♕xd5+ cxd5 41 ♖g1 ♖e3 42 ♘c1 d4 43 ♘b3 a4 White resigns.**

123. I see a different way of expressing moves in old books. Why is that?

In English-language chess literature, the dominant style was something called Descriptive Notation. There is a similar version in older Spanish books and magazines.

In Descriptive Notation, squares were identified differently from White's viewpoint and Black's. For instance, an opening would be written as **1 P-K4 P-K4 2 N-KB3 N-QB3 3 B-N5 N-B3 4 BxN.** The Algebraic version of the same moves is **1 e4 e5 2 ♘f3 ♘c6 3 ♗b5 ♘f6 4 ♗xc6.**

Algebraic drove Descriptive out of fashion in the final decades of the 20th century but there are many high-quality books that were never converted to Algebraic.

124. Are there different versions of Algebraic?

There are several minor differences and some major variations.

Minor differences include omitting the captures sign (4 ♗c6 in the last example). Among the major variations is the long form (1 e2-e4 e7-e5 2 ♘g1-f3 ♘b8-c6).

You don't even need to identify the pieces, just the squares they move from and to (2 g1-f3 b8-c6 3 f1-b5).

Experienced players have learned to understand all of these, even those used by computers.

125. Are computers ever wrong in analysis?

Yes, they still have blind spots.

They are infallible in database endgames. But add a pawn or two and they can declare a rook endgame to be winning when an average experienced player knows it is very drawish.

In general, computers are right. But relying on them to answer your questions is a bad habit.

126. Why?

Because you are cheating yourself out of a lesson. If you see a position that you don't understand, try to figure it yourself. Computers should be a last resort.

71

Besides, a computer can tell you which is the best move and second-best in a position. But it may not tell you why.

If you don't understand the reason a move is good and another move is better, the computer is little help.

127. Which Web sites are good for training?

There are many you should take a look at. Among them Chess.com, Internet chess club.com, Lichess.org, Chess24.com., 365chess.com, Chessgames.com. and Chesstempo.com.

128. What about DVDs and podcasts?

They can be excellent. There is plenty of material waiting for you, such as tutorials on Youtube.

But there is a danger. By watching a screen you become a passive participant.

You can easily feel detached, the way you do when watching television and a commercial comes on. You are still watching but not engaged. How much of a TV commercial do you remember once it is off the screen?

When Garry Kasparov played an Internet game against the "World," some three million viewers watched his game. But on a typical day about one tenth of one percent of the viewers voted to choose a move.

Masters who grew up reading chess books said they made it an active experience. They often disagreed with the author's conclusions, checked his analysis on a board and pieces, wrote notes in pencil in the book.

Yasser Seirawan's approach to published analysis when he was young was to act "incredibly negative" towards it.

"You're wrong," he would imagine saying to the annotator. "Then I try to prove that I'm right." This follows his "any analysis you do is good" credo.

129. Do I need a teacher to make progress?

Emanuel Lasker reflected a common view when he said, "Properly taught, a student can learn more in a few hours than in 10 years of untutored trial and error."

But Lasker's only real teacher was his older brother. There have been many great players who never took a lesson – or taught one, for that matter. Mikhail Botvinnik became a great teacher but his mantra was "Chess can't be taught. It can only be learned."

130. What does that mean?

It means you learn best when you learn independently, on your own.

Botvinnik ran a celebrated school for talented youngsters. But it was a correspondence school. He only met with his students a few times a year, to review their homework. The learning happened in the homework, he said.

131. What can a teacher do for me?

Good teachers are guides, not lecturers.

They ask a student questions about a position rather than give answers. They appraise a student's weakness and strengths and then recommend a plan for the student's independent study.

132. Does my teacher have to be a grandmaster?

No. If someone created a hall of fame for greatest teachers, there would be few grandmasters inside.

Good teachers are experienced players who have also a lot of experience teaching. Bobby Fischer, Mikhail Tal, Tigran Petrosian, Boris Spassky and many others spoke very highly of their first teachers – none of whom were grandmasters.

133. How do I know that I'm really learning?

You probably won't. At least, not when it is happening.

Much – if not most – of what you learn about chess will be subliminal and incremental. It will be added slowly to what you already know.

Chess is really several different subjects – tactics, endgame technique, pawn play, openings, and so on. Only in some of the simpler subjects can you be sure you are learning. For example, you can try to win the basic mate of king and two bishops against king, playing against a computer.

White to play and mate

If you can do it without becoming frustrated and quit, this shows what you've learned. You can do it again and see if you can mate in fewer moves. (Databases say it can be done in 15 moves.)

But basic endgames are one of the few subjects that you can be certain you have mastered.

134. How can I know that I've mastered a tougher subject?

One good method is show-and-tell:

Imagine that you are a teacher and you are explaining something to an imaginary student. Pick something that you've just learned.

Dominguez – Carlsen

Internet 2021

Black to move

Look up this kind of position from a textbook. When you think you understand it, try explaining it to your phantom student.

You might say:

"Most bishop endgames with just one pawn are a draw with best play. But this is different because White can be prevented from giving up his bishop after …a2.

"Black's winning method is to get his bishop to a2. He did that with **68…♗g6 69 ♗e6 ♗b1 70 ♗d5 ♗a2!**.

"A trade of bishops is an easy win, 71 ♗xa2 ♔xa2 and 71…♔b2, 73…a2.

Therefore 71 ♗e4 ♗f7 and White had one last trick, 72 ♗b1!"

Black to move

"He would draw after 72...♔xb1?? 73 ♔xa3.

But he had no good moves after **72...♗b3!.**

He resigned in view of 73 ♔-moves ♔xb1 or 73 ♗e4 a2."

If you can explain all that, you've gotten a pretty good grip on the subject.

But this takes time. Don't expect "Eureka moments."

135. What are those?

They happen when you suddenly realize you can apply something you learned. Suppose you find yourself in a king and pawn ending. You can't see a way to win it. Then you remember triangulation (see Question 418). You play the right moves and you win. It's a great feeling.

But there are very few experiences like that.

A university professor, Stuart Dreyfus, wondered why he failed to become a chess master after considerable effort. He studied how people became experts in various fields, including chess masters.

One of his conclusions is that chess knowledge comes without your being aware that it is happening.

"You know something without knowing how you know it," he wrote in *Mind over Machine.*

Every chess master can say that happened to them.

Chapter Seven: Evaluating

136. Why is it important to evaluate a position?

When you choose a move to play, you want to know whether it improves your winning chances. But you can't know this unless you compare the consequences of that move with the consequences of other moves.

Opponents constantly evaluate moves in a game. They often come to the same conclusion – up to a point.

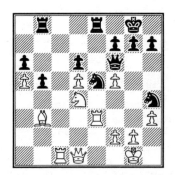

Vachier-Lagrave – Dubov

Internet 2020

White to move

White chose **27 ♘c6** after considering the ways Black can meet the threat of 28 ♘xb8.

He had foreseen, for example, that 27...♘xc6 would allow him to create a very powerful passed pawn with 28 ♖xe8+ and 29 dxc6!.

After White played 27 ♘c6, Black also concluded 27...♘xc6? would be bad.

He opted for the complex **27...♘xf5,** after seeing how good 28 ♘xb8? ♘xe3 was.

White agreed he was right about that evaluation. Play continued **28 ♖xe5 dxe5 29 ♘xb8 ♖xb8**. So far, so good.

137. What happens when two good players don't agree on the evaluation?

The one who is right usually wins. That was the case when the last example reached this position.

White to move

White believed he was much better because of **30 ♖c6!**. He could safely win a pawn after 30...♘d6 31 ♖xa6.

Black believed he would be doing well once he played ...♘d4.

For example, 30...♕d8 31 ♖xa6 ♘d4! followed by ...♖a8.

But Black had misevaluated what happens after **30...♕d8** is met by **31 d6!**. This opened up the business diagonal of White's bishop.

After **31...♘d4 32 ♖xa6 b4 33 ♖a7!** White threatened to capture on f7 and soon won.

138. Is it realistic to evaluate a position based on the best moves being played?

Flawless chess does not exist, even in computer versus computer games.

But you can't evaluate the consequences of a move accurately unless you consider the best replies by your opponent. This means the worst outcome for you.

So – Vachier-Lagrave

Internet 2020

White to move

The safety-minded 44 ♔h1! would get out of the second-rank pin and threaten to win with 45 ♗xf3+. Chances would be roughly equal.

But White played **44 ♖b1**. How do we evaluate it?

Is it good because it threatens to win with 45 ♕b6+ ?

Is it the best move because Black would lose after 44…b5 45 ♕a8+ ?

No. It should be judged on the basis of the worst-case scenario. Black has only one good move. But it is **44…♖xg2+!** so that **45 ♔xg2 ♖xg3+!**.

Then 46 ♔xg3 ♕g6+ and …♕xb1 reaches a winning queen endgame.

It didn't matter how many other scenarios were favorable for White after 44 ♖b1??. Only the worst case counted.

139. How do annotators indicate how advantageous a position is?

They often use symbols. A plus sign over an equals sign means a slight edge for White. If the equals sign sits above the plus sign, it means the opposite, a slight edge for Black.

For a greater advantage, it is a plus sign followed by a dash. Some authors use "+ -" to mean White has a distinct advantage and others use it to mean White is winning.

140. What if there is just an equal sign? Does that mean a draw is likely?

Not at all. It just means there are equal opportunities to win.

You will also hear the term "double-edged position." This is a cliché that means there are good winning chances for each player and a somewhat low likelihood of a draw.

Radjabov – Nepomniachtchi

Internet 2020

Black to move

Black is about to make a crucial choice. After 35…♗d4 he would threaten 36…♕xe4. Then 36 ♖c2 ♗xc5 leaves the winning chances balanced.

Black preferred **35…♕h4** and the position became more double-edged.

Of course, a draw is still possible. But there are many more ways for either player to go wrong.

White replied **36 ♔e1**.

Black to move

A rook retreat such as 37...♖d8 would threaten to win with 38...♕h1+.

But this would favor White after 38 ♖g5!.

Instead, Black played **36...♖b2!**.

Chances continued to be equal. A draw might come about after 37 fxe5 ♕h1+ 38 ♕f1 ♕h4! and then 39 ♕d3 ♕h1+, repeating the position.

But the losing chances had continued to rise. White blundered with **37 ♖g3??**.

He resigned after **37 ...♕h2! 38 ♗g2 ♕g1+ 39 ♗f1 ♕xf2+**.

141. How slight is a "slight advantage"?

Like many common chess expressions this has no exact definition.

It could something like a 55 to 65 percent chance of winning.

Masters use adjectives such as "significant" or "solid" or "major" for an advantage above that.

It becomes a "winning advantage" around 90 percent – and a forced win at 100 percent.

142. Do computers evaluate positions in terms of winning percent?

With the notable exception of AlphaZero, they express evaluations in plus and minus numbers.

For example, a +2.00 advantage means a White advantage equivalent to two extra pawns. This is usually enough to win.

Esipenko – Carlsen

Wijk aan Zee 2021

Black to move

Here computers render evaluations ranging from +1.20 to +2.00.

The numbers soon doubled as White eliminated Black's counterplay, **25...♕e8 26 ♖g5 ♖a4 27 ♖a5 ♖ab4 28 b3 ♖4b7 29 ♕c3 ♕d8 30 ♗f3.** This turned out to be a stunning upset of the world champion.

143. What positional factors go into evaluation?

Everything besides material.

In the last example, White had an extra pawn. That could mean a +1.00 advantage.

But his three passed queenside pawns added to it because it meant an endgame would be easily won.

In quieter positions, having the better bishop, rook control of an open file, superior pawn structure and so on are positional plusses. It gets confusing when one player has some assets and his opponent has others.

144. If assets offset one another how does anyone know how big an advantage there is?

This may sound surprising, but there is no consensus about how to precisely evaluate positions.

There is general agreement that material and king safety are the two most important criteria. But some authorities say material is No. 1 and others say the king safety is.

After that comes piece power – the mobility and cooperation of your pieces. This is followed by how much space you control, the condition of your pawns and some sophisticated criteria such as the ability to improve your chances.

145. How does mobility matter?

Mobility means the range your pieces enjoy: How many squares can they go to on the next move?

For instance, you can get a rough idea of who stands better in a rook endgame if you count the pawns. But if pawns are equal, count the number of possible rook moves. Whoever has the more active rook usually has the upper hand.

But it is easy to overrate mobility before the pieces are fully engaged in play.

For example, a standard variation of the Ruy Lopez begins **1 e4 e5 2 ♘f3 ♘c6 3 ♗b5 a6 4 ♗a4 ♘f6 5 0-0 ♗e7 6 ♖e1 b5 7 ♗b3 d6 8 c3 0-0 9 h3 ♘a5 10 ♗c2**.

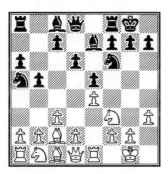

Black to move

Computers once preferred Black's chances because of his superior mobility. Two of White's queenside pieces, the c1-bishop and rook, have no legal moves. His b1-knight has one.

Yet the experience of tens of thousands of games assures us that White has the better prospects.

Once the middlegame begins, piece power can also be gauged by how well a player's pieces are coordinated. That is, how well they protect one another and attack common squares.

Both mobility and coordination are closely related to control of space.

146. Why is space important?

The player who has access to more of the board's squares, especially center squares, has the greater options in the middlegame.

This is ancient wisdom, but a young Anatoly Karpov discounted it when he played in his first Olympiad team tournament.

Hase – Karpov
Skopje 1972

1 e4 e5 2 d4 exd4 3 ♕xd4 ♘c6 4 ♕e3 d6?

The Center Game has been a discredited opening for a century. But it is easy to underestimate the value of White's advantage in space.

5. ♘c3 ♘f6 6 ♗d2 ♗e7 7 0-0-0! 0-0 8 ♕g3 a6 9 f4 b5 10 e5 ♘d7 11 ♘f3 ♖b8

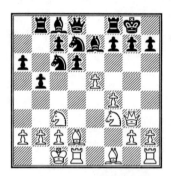

White to move

Now 12 ♗e3 and ♗d3 would assure White clearly superior prospects.

A space advantage is based on pawn structure and it lasts longer than piece mobility. In many popular openings – such as the Sicilian, King's Indian, Queen's Indian and Nimzo-Indian defenses – White can post pieces and pawns on his first four ranks. Black often has nothing beyond the third rank.

This situation often lasts well past move 20. By then White's advantage in time is usually gone. But his space edge persists.

147. What does a time advantage mean?

This is one of the key differences between chess and military strategy. Armies don't take turns attacking. The army that can make one attacking move after another has the upper hand.

In chess, we count time in moves and call them tempi. A player who begins a game with 1 ♘f3 and 2 ♘g1? has wasted two tempi.

An advantage in time is temporary. It is only valuable if you use it. For example, there is a rule of thumb that says a pawn can be sacrificed in the opening in return for at least three tempi.

A variation of the Catalan Opening, **1 d4 d5 2 c4 e6 3 ♘f3 ♘f6 4 g3 dxc4 5 ♗g2 a6 6 0-0 b5**, goes **7 ♘e5 ♘d5 8 a4 c6 9 e4 ♘f6**.

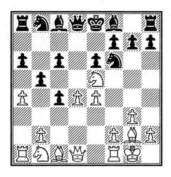

White to move

White has a big edge in both time and space. He can exploit them with **10 d5!**.

For example, 10...cxd5 11 exd5 exd5 12 axb5 with advantage.

148. Why doesn't a time advantage last?

The player who is ahead in development typically runs out of moves that significantly improve his chances.

His opponent catches up. By the endgame, time is rarely a factor.

Time was once considered much more important than it is today. Siegbert Tarrasch claimed that the loss of a single move of development was a bad mistake.

He gave the example of **1 e4 e5 2 ♘f3 ♘f6 3 ♘xe5 d6 4 ♘f3 ♘xe4 5 ♕e2 ♕e7 6 d3 ♘f6 7 ♗g5**.

Tarrasch said **7...♕xe2+** deserved a question mark because after **8 ♗xe2** White has gained a free developing move (♗e2).

Black to move

But experience has shown that an extra tempo means little once queens are off the board. Black is worse after 8...♗e7 9 ♘c3 c6 but not by much.

What happened in Vladimir Kramnik's first world championship match is instructive. When he was Black he steered play into an endgame, in the Berlin Defense of the Ruy Lopez.

His opponent, Garry Kasparov, held a small advantage in time and space in each of the four games in which this happened. But he drew all four games and this effectively cost him his championship title.

149. What about king safety? Is having the more secure king a big plus?

Chess is a zero-sum game in many ways: If you are ahead in material, your opponent must be behind by the same amount.

But in other cases, the arithmetic doesn't add up. If your opponent's king is exposed and vulnerable to attack, this is a big plus for you. But if both kings are safe – and your king is better protected than his – it doesn't change the evaluation much.

150. How important is the ability to improve a position?

It varies quite a bit, as this extreme example will show:

White to move

This illustrates one of the few ways we are still superior to computers. Some engines claim a huge White advantage, of more than +15.

They suggest ways to improve it, such as 1 0-0-0, 2 ♗d3, 3 ♖h3, 4 ♔d2.

But it is evident to humans that White cannot penetrate the pawn wall. If he plays ♖h4, for example, Black just ignores it.

151. Which components of evaluation last the longest?

A material advantage. It can only change due to a capture.

Pawn weaknesses come next in longevity. Doubled, isolated pawns tend to remain double and isolated.

Next comes king safety. An exposed king can be far more important than an extra piece. But given time, a king can scurry to a haven.

Piece placement is a relatively short-lived value. A protected knight on a central square can be traded off. The rook that commands an open file can be challenged by another rook. Even a bad bishop might improve by maneuvering.

152. Is having the initiative an advantage?

This is tricky because there is no generally accepted definition of the initiative.

If we agree that it means the ability to make threats, then the initiative is an advantage. But it is temporary. The threats can end.

World Champion José Capablanca believed the initiative was inherently advantageous. But he meant being able to make threats for several moves.

153. Are there other criteria that a computer can't evaluate?

Yes. A prime example is playability.

A position that is more playable for one player than for his opponent means that he will have an easier time finding good moves.

It can also mean that there will be more ways for his opponent to err.

Karjakin – Carlsen

World Championship match 2016

Black to move

Computers list a variety of good options for Black but none of them leads to a superior position.

Black chose **30...e4!** and this move more than any other won the world championship match. Play continued **31 dxe4 ♗xc3 32 ♖xc3 ♛e5**.

Black's chances have gotten worse, according to many engines. But Carlsen understood that it had become much harder for White to find good moves and much easier for him to find them.

White to move

The game ended with **33 ♖c1 ♖a8 34 h3 h6 35 ♔h2 ♕d4 36 ♕e1? ♕b2! 37 ♗f1 ♖a2! 38. ♖xc7?? ♖a1 White resigns**.

Don't confuse playability with the term "playable." When an annotator says a move is playable, he means that it isn't a mistake and the resulting position is tenable.

154. Can both players think they have the advantage?

Yes, and that's another reason chess fascinates us.

White may like his kingside attacking chances, but Black may believe he will survive the attack and win an endgame.

The reverse is possible. Both players can think they stand badly.

Chess players are prone to be either optimists or pessimists. Only computers are immune.

Chapter Eight: Trading

155. I can't attack without my queen and other pieces. Why should I want to trade them?

Attacking is one of the three basic ways of winning a chess game. The other two are amassing a material edge and accumulating positional assets. A good trade can improve your chances of success in all three ways.

156. But trades are just trades. How do they help me win?

There is often a subtle difference between the traded pieces.

If you swap a passive knight for a well-posted knight, this is a plus. So is trading a "bad" bishop for a good one.

From the opening to the endgame you are probably going to make four or five trades of one piece for an identical piece. If two or three of the exchanges are favorable, it adds up.

Ivkov – Hort

Varna 1962

White to move

White can try to improve his pieces by doubling rooks on the d-file or attacking the queenside (24 a4).

But his superiority became clearer after he exchanged two pairs of identical pieces, **24 ♘xd6 ♖xd6 25 ♖xd6 ♕xd6**.

After a forcing move, **26 ♖d1**, he could prepare another trade, of queens.

There followed **26...♕c6 27 ♕d3 c4 28 ♕d7 ♕xd7 29 ♖xd7**.

Black to move

The three trades left White with a substantial advantage in piece power.

Black had passive pieces and could not put up much resistance: **29...♘c6 30 g5 ♗h5 31 ♔g3 ♔g8 32 f3 ♔f8 33 ♖b7 ♔e8 34 a4 ♖b8 35 ♖c7 ♘d8 36 ♖a7 b4 37 a5 b3 38 ♗d1 resigns** before ♖xa6 and ♗e2xc4.

157. Are there guidelines for making good trades?

Yes, and common sense tells you the simplest – Trade inferior pieces for better enemy pieces and trade when you are ahead in material.

The other important ones are:

a) Trade when your pieces are cramped.

b) What stays on the board is more important that what goes off.

c) Trading increases in significance as the game goes on.

158. Why would my opponent allow me to trade off his good piece for my inferior one?

You can make him an offer he can't refuse.

This may happen very early in the game. For example, **1 e4 e6 2 d4 d5 3 e5** and now **3...b6 4 ♘f3 ♗a6**.

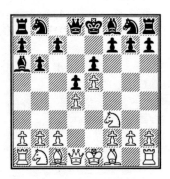

White to move

Black's light-squared bishop was slightly inferior to White's after 1...e6 and 2...d5. Black's last move forced a trade of them.

This particular trade is double-edged. White can gain valuable time and misplace Black's knight with 5 ♗xa6 ♘xa6 and then threaten it (with 6 c4! followed by 7 ♕a4+ and ♕xa6).

Nevertheless, ridding yourself of your worst pieces – usually minor pieces – is a valuable skill. When Russian players were studying how to beat Bobby Fischer, one of them exclaimed, "Do you realize he never has any bad pieces? He exchanges them, and the bad ones remain with his opponents."

159. I can't evaluate good and bad pieces when the game has just started. Is there another reason to trade them?

Yes, the guideline about cramped pieces.

Black typically has less space in the opening, as we talked about in Question 146. Swapping just one pair of knights can change that.

An illustration is **1 e4 g6 2 d4 ♗g7 3 ♘f3 d6 4 c3 ♘f6 5 ♘bd2 0-0 6 ♗d3 ♘c6 7 0-0 e5 8 dxe5**.

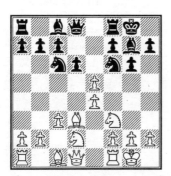

Black to move

The natural 8...dxe5 favors White slightly after 9 ♘c4. For example, 9...♕e7 10 b4 with the idea of b4-b5 and ♗a3. Or 9...♖e8 10 ♕c2 and ♖d1.

But Black has an easier middlegame after **9...♘xe5!** and then **10 ♘xe5 dxe5**. For instance 11 ♘c4 ♕e7 or 11...♘h5.

160. I don't understand "What stays on the board is more important than what goes off."

This is an insight from Siegbert Tarrasch. It explains why trading a good piece for an inferior one may make sense:

Don't evaluate a trade solely in terms of the departing pieces. You should also pay attention to the pieces that remain.

In the diagram of Question 156, the White knight on f5 and his rooks were better than Black's knight on d6 and his rooks. But White superiority shone through only after three swaps. Here's another example.

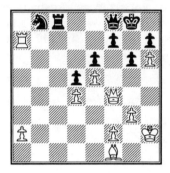

Kamsky – Lenderman

St. Louis 2014

White to move

After 46 a4, Black would be worse but can put up resistance with 46...♞a5.

However, he could safely resign after **46 ♗b5!**.

The reason is that when he plays ...♞c6, White will respond ♗xc6!.

The bishop is better than the knight. But after **46...♞c6 47 ♗xc6! ♖xc6 48 ♔g2:**

Black to move

White has a simple winning plan of pushing his a-pawn. If Black stops it, he allows something equally bad.

For example, 48...♖c4 49 ♕f6 ♖c8 (49...♖xd4 50 ♖a8! and ♕g7 mate) 50 a4 ♖b8 51 a5 ♖c8 52 a6 ♖b8 53 ♖b7 ♖a8 54 a7 and 55 ♖b8.

In view of this, Black resigned.

161. *Are there guidelines for when I should avoid a trade?*

When you are behind in material, try to keep pieces on the board.

But trade as many pawns as you can. Endgames are typically won by promoting a pawn. The fewer pawns left, the more likely that the inferior side can draw.

One other tip: It often pays to retreat a piece rather than allow it to be exchanged. This can happen early in a game.

162. *How early?*

Very. A retreat in the opening can help you build a spatial advantage.

For example, **1 c4 c5 2 ♘c3 ♘f6 3 g3 d5 4 cxd5 ♘xd5 5 ♗g2**.

Black to move

Black's knight is attacked and 5...♘xc3 6 bxc3 helps White build a strong pawn center after d2-d4.

The best option is **5...♘c7!**.

This hands White a lead in development, **6 ♘f3 ♘c6 7 0-0**.

However, Black controls more key central squares after **7...e5!**

White to move

He enjoys an advantage in space. He can occupy his first four ranks while White can be limited to the three closest to him.

White has an advantage in time but cannot exploit it. Once Black catches up in development, he will have a fine game.

For example, 8 d3 ♝e7 9 ♝e3 0-0 10 ♖c1 ♝e6.

163. Which pieces are usually traded first in a game?

Knights usually go first and rooks go last.

For example, Black's b8-knight was gone from the board in about three quarters of the final positions of games in a massive database.

But most games end with at least one rook on the board. Queens are next in terms of longevity.

164. Why are knights traded so quickly?

There are three reasons. First, knights are typically developed before other pieces and that makes them more vulnerable to capture.

Second, a knight is best placed in or near the center of the board. That also makes it more subject to a trade.

Third, a knight can be swapped for any of four enemy pieces of equal value. That is more than the other pieces:

A queen can be identically swapped for only one piece, the other queen. A rook can be traded equally for either of two enemy rooks. A bishop can be swapped directly for one of three minor pieces. (But not for an opposite-colored bishop.)

It is worth noting that a BxB trade changes the thinking of the two players more than a NxN trade.

165. How is that?

The first swap of bishop for bishop can help you decide where to put your pawns. Generally, you want them on squares of the color of the bishop you no longer have.

For example, after **1 e4 c5 2 ♘f3 d6** there is a variation that runs **3 ♝b5+ ♝d7 4 ♝xd7+ ♛xd7** and now **5 0-0 ♘c6 6 c3 ♘f6 7 ♖e1.**

The trade tells both players that the light-squared center squares are more valuable because there are fewer enemy pieces to contest their control.

The right way to deal with this is **7…e6!** and then **8 d4 cxd4 9 cxd4 d5!.**

White to move

Now the light squares are secure for Black. White has no advantage after 10 exd5 ♘xd5 or 11 e5 ♘e4.

166. Can one piece trade encourage me to make another?

Yes. Suppose you trade a bishop for a knight and as a result your opponent has "the two bishops." That's a slight material advantage for him.

But if you swap your remaining bishop for one of his, his "two bishop" edge is gone. (Remember Question 30?)

167. Which piece trades should I spend time learning about?

Bishops, for the reasons just mentioned, and queens because of how transformative it is to go into an endgame.

As you make more exchanges in your playing career, you'll learn how unequal most "equal" trades can be.

Chapter Nine: Openings

168. Is there a best opening move?

There is no such thing.

You should find the move that is easiest for you to play. Most newcomers to chess find 1 e4 fits the bill.

169. But don't masters strongly favor one opening move over another?

They did, a long time ago.

For most of the period 1600-1900, they preferred 1 e4. Then so many strong players switched to 1 d4 that 1 e4 was nearly driven out of master chess.

170. Was that because 1 e4 was refuted?

No. Opening preference is more fashion than science.

Masters turned to 1 d4 because there was less known about it than about 1 e4. Then 1 c4 and 1 ♘f3 became trendy.

Today, many of the world's best players are comfortable with any of those four most popular moves.

Magnus Carlsen has even played – and won – with moves that were once considered ridiculous: 1 a3, 1 c3, 1 ♘c3 and 1 ♘h3. For example: **1 a3 g6 2 h4 h5**

Carlsen – Holm

Internet 2018

White to move

Carlsen typically outplays weaker opponents, even grandmasters, in the middlegame. Here he is seeking an opening position in which both players have to think for themselves.

3 e4 c5 4 ♗c4 ♗g7 5 ♘c3 ♘c6 6 ♘f3 d6 7 ♘g5 e6 8 d3 ♘ge7 9 ♗a2 ♘d4 10 ♘e2 ♘ec6 11 ♘f4 ♘e5 12 c3

White has a small advantage, which is all Carlsen really wanted.

12...♘dc6 13 f3 ♕b6 14 ♕e2 ♕a5 15 ♗d2 ♕b5 16 ♗e3 b6 17 0-0 0-0 18 a4 ♕a6 19 ♕d2 ♕a5 20 ♕f2 ♕a6 21 ♖fd1 ♘e7? 22 d4! cxd4 23 cxd4 ♘c4 24 ♗xc4 ♕xc4 25 ♖dc1 ♕a6 26 ♖c7! ♖e8 27 ♘xf7! ♔xf7 28 ♕g3 ♔f6 29 ♕g5+ ♔f7 30 ♘xg6 ♗f6 31 ♕xh5 ♔g7 32 ♗h6+ ♔g8 33 ♘xe7+ ♖xe7 34 ♕g6+ resigns

171. Which first moves are easiest to learn?

Easiest are 1 e4 as White and meeting it with 1...e5 as Black.

There is no better way to learn basic opening principles, especially rapid development and respect for the center.

The positions that derive from these moves also teach the kind of tactics that help you the most when you are starting out in chess.

After you become a better player, there are plenty of other openings to adopt. But 1 e4 and 1...e5 are a good way to begin.

172. How much of an advantage is it to have White?

Less than you think.

Several databases of master games indicate White comes out ahead roughly 52 to 55 percent of the time.

That is, in 100-game match between two masters, White would score about 52 to 55 points.

Bear in mind, masters are good at maintaining an opening advantage. When non-masters play, the benefit of making the first move often becomes trivial.

173. Why do many players study openings more than anything else?

Two main reasons:

First, you can immediately apply what you study. You can learn enough about the French Defense in one weekend to play it with some confidence in your next game.

In contrast, you can master bishop endgames and not get a chance to use your knowledge in the next year.

Second, the more you know about a particular opening, the later in a game you have to start thinking.

174. Don't chess players like to think?

Absolutely. But they like chess more when they can make an opening move that forces their opponent to do the *first* thinking of the game.

If your opponent's knowledge of an opening ends at Move Eight – and you can rely on your memory for a few more moves, this is a big head start.

It can also be a psychological weapon. You can "blitz" opening moves to intimidate opponents.

Blitzing happens at many rating levels and it is particularly powerful in the hands of grandmasters who prepare their openings in enormous depth.

Caruana – Alekseenko
Candidates tournament 2020

1 d4 ♘f6 2 c4 e6 3 ♘c3 ♗b4 4 f3 d5 5 a3 ♗e7 6 e4 dxe4 7 fxe4 c5 8 d5 exd5 9 exd5 0-0 10 ♗e2 ♖e8 11 ♘f3 ♗g4 12 0-0 ♘bd7 13 d6 ♗f8 14 h3

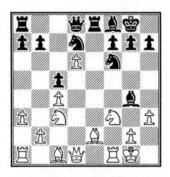

Black to move

The two players had taken only a few minutes to play their first 13 moves. But 14 h3 was new to Black.

It isn't a particularly powerful move. Its punch lies in its novelty. Black spent nearly an hour on his next two moves, **14...♗h5 15 ♘b5 ♖e6?**.

The position quickly went from balanced to solidly in White's favor: **16 ♗f4 a6 17 ♘c7 ♖e4 18 ♗h2 ♖c8 19 g4** and this became critical after **19...♗xg4 20 hxg4 ♘xg4 21 ♗d3 ♘xh2 22 ♗xe4 ♘xf1 23 ♕xf1 ♗xd6 24 ♘d5 g6 25 ♕h3** – because Black only had five minutes left.

White had more than an hour more and soon won.

175. I can't blitz. What should I be doing in the opening?

Your top three priorities are the ones that every beginner is taught:

Develop your pieces.

Control center squares.

Make your king safe for the coming middlegame.

After that comes maximizing the mobility and coordination of your pieces.

In the early days of computer chess, programmers built this into rules of thumb called heuristics. But they found it difficult to add other guidelines, such as "Don't develop a piece on a bad or vulnerable square."

176. Why?

For the same reason that plagues humans: There are too many variables in chess. Guidelines are bound to contradict one another.

For instance, after **1 e4 e5 2 d4 exd4 3 ♕xd4** the queen is developed and controls all of the center squares.

That should be good. But the queen comes under immediate attack, **3...♘c6!**.

Then Black can take over control of key center squares, such as after **4 ♕a4 ♘f6 5 ♘c3 ♗c5**.

White to move

Black already has the better development, as **6 ♘f3 ♘g4 7 ♘d1 0-0** indicates. White had lost some time with 3 ♕xd4.

177. What other guidelines are worth knowing?

There are several, starting with:

Developing a piece is better than moving an already developed piece.

The best square for a piece is one that will not obstruct other pieces or be easily attacked by a weaker piece.

Castling is a developing move that also brings the king to safety.

Bring out at least one knight – and preferably both – before you develop both of your bishops. This is known as "Knights before bishops."

178. Why does "Knights before bishops" make sense?

"You know where the knight belongs before you know much about your bishop," as Wilhelm Steinitz, the first official world champion, put it.

What he meant is that the best squares for a bishop usually depend on the pawn structure. But knights can find good squares before the pawn structure is formed.

One of the few legitimate openings in which White first develops both bishops while Black develops knights is **1 e4 e5 2 ♗c4 ♘f6 3 d3 ♘c6 4 ♗g5.**

Black to move

Black can get a comfortable game with **4...h6!**.

For example, **5 ♗h4 g5 6 ♗g3 d5!** and he has the greater play in the center.

White's g3-bishop can be buried by Black pawns after 7 exd5 ♘xd5 8 ♘f3 ♗g7 9 0-0 0-0 and ...f5.

There is another reason for "Knights before bishops." It follows the principle of preserving your greater options.

179. What is the reasoning for that?

Common sense. You should do the things you are *likely* to do before choosing among the things you *might* do.

This means the first pieces to develop should be those that have the fewest good places to land.

For example, White plays ♘f3 in most games because the knight is rarely well-placed on h3 and not often well-placed on e2.

His kingside bishop has greater options. It may serve best on c4 – or b5, g2, d3 and e2, depending on Black's moves. Therefore, White can wait before choosing a bishop move.

The principle of preserving options works best in the opening, less so in the middlegame and rarely in the endgame.

180. Can I rely on common sense for most opening moves?

World Champion Emanuel Lasker claimed you could, in a book titled *Common Sense in Chess*. But he was stretching the truth for the benefit of novices.

The best moves often look strange, if not illogical. A major opening begins **1 e4 e6 2 d4 d5 3 ♘c3 ♗b4 4 e5 c5 5 a3 ♗xc3+ 6 bxc3 ♘e7**.

White to move

There is a natural developing move, **7 ♘f3**. It is often followed by another, ♗d3 or ♗e2.

But masters also like sophisticated moves that you won't easily arrive at via common sense, such as **7 h4** and **7 a4**.

The most popular move is **7 ♕g4**, which violates general principles by advancing the queen before any other pieces.

Chess has its own strange logic, and players often bend it to justify their latest opinion. Bobby Fischer was a lifelong 1 e4 player. But at the very end of that life he said, "1 d4 is better!"

Why? "Because the pawn on d4 is protected," he said.

181. Is there a best time for me to study openings?

You learn best when you are motivated most. And you will never be as motivated to learn about an opening than after you've just played it in a game you took seriously.

Don't throw the moment away by excusing what happened. Don't say, "I never play well against the Caro-Kann." Or "That's the last time I'm going into the Evans Gambit."

Instead, look up the opening moves in a book or database. See what you did wrong. Figure out how you would play differently the next time you get that position.

182. Suppose I want to learn a new opening. How do I start?

A good way to begin is to look at several games of an opening that piqued your interest. You can start with an online database, such as chessgames.com.

Suppose you want to see if the King's Gambit suits you. Search for games that begin with the gambit moves, 1 e4 e5 2 f4. Click through a few of them. They don't have to be grandmaster games. Don't try to analyze them in depth. You want to get a taste of them. For example:

Ivanchuk – Leko
Internet 2020

1 e4 e5 2 f4 exf4 3 ♘f3 h6 4 d4 g5 5 g3 fxg3 6 hxg3 ♗g7 7 ♘c3 d6 8 ♗e3 ♘f6 9 ♕d2 ♘g4 10 ♗g1 ♘c6 11 0-0-0

Black to move

You want to ask questions when you look at games like this:

Is the White position something I would enjoy playing? Do I like the tactical middlegames that 2 f4 leads to?

If the answers are "No," take a look at another opening, such as 2 ♘c3 or 2 ♗c4.

In this case, White won, although chances were in balance after **11…0-0 12 ♘h2 ♘xh2 13 ♖xh2 ♗g4 14 ♖e1 ♘e7 15 ♗g2 ♕d7 16. ♗e3 ♘g6 17 ♖eh1 c6 18 ♖xh6 ♗xh6 19 ♖xh6**.

Don't get discouraged if you decide you don't like an opening. There are dozens of others. There has to be one for you.

183. How many Black openings should I know?

You need one good answer to 1 d4. This is sufficient for the vast majority of players.

The easiest reply to learn is 1…d5. If 2 c4, then 2…e6, the Queen's Gambit Declined.

This also provides a foundation for learning how to handle other non-1 e4 openings. For instance, you can answer 1 c4 with 1…e6 and 2…d5 and get positions similar to 1 d4 d5 ones.

184. How many defenses do masters learn?

They like to have two or three defenses to every major opening move by White. This allows them to vary their opening, depending on their opponent, their mood and so on.

After 1 e4, they can choose among a solid defense such as 1…e5, a more enterprising one, 1…c5, and a more conservative one such as 1…e6 or 1…c6.

What masters rarely admit is that all major openings are good at the amateur level.

As Grandmaster Bent Larsen said, "If you are not a master it is stupid to learn many openings." There's just too much "book."

185. What do you mean by "book"?

A book move is one that has occurred often enough in master games to be regarded as the best in that particular position. The term comes from the day when only the moves published in books were respected.

101

When a master annotates a game in which a rare or original move is played he may refer to the alternative by saying, "The book move is…" or "Theory recommends…"

186. Is "theory" different from "book"?

"Theory" may be temporary. It is the consensus view at the moment. It changes when masters find better moves.

GM Lev Alburt recalled analyzing an opening with Mikhail Botvinnik and saying that "theory recommends" a particular move.

Botvinnik corrected him: "Lev, we are theory, you and I."

187. So there is nothing theoretical about "theory"?

No, this is another confusing chess term. Opening theory is actually opening experience or opening practice.

And there is nothing theoretical about "endgame theory." This is also book knowledge, about commonly occurring endgames. But its verdict about the best moves is rarely changed because of a new discovery.

188. Do good players ever deliberately play bad opening moves?

Yes, when they try to win quickly by setting traps.

The first game Beth Harmon plays in the TV series *The Queen's Gambit* begins **1 e4 e5 2 ♗c4 ♘c6** and her opponent plays **3 ♕f3?**.

This exposes the queen too early. But Beth tries to punish it with **3…♘d4??** and the game ends with **4 ♕xf7 mate**.

This is an ancient trap, sometimes set with 3 ♕h5. It is known as the Scholar's Mate and, more appropriately, the Children's Mate.

Mikhail Tal said that after falling into it against a relative he decided to take chess seriously.

189. Are traps always set by bad moves?

No, quite a few come naturally out of sound openings. A common one begins **1 d4 d5 2 c4 e6 3 ♘c3 ♘f6 4 ♗g5 ♘bd7 5 cxd5 exd5**.

White to move

Now **6 ♘xd5?** loses a piece to **6...♘xd5! 7 ♗xd8 ♗b4+** because Black regains his queen, with interest.

But 4...♘bd7 should not be considered a trap. It is simply a book move with the usual good attributes.

190. I heard someone say a move "transposes." What did he mean?

Several opening positions can arise from a different order of moves. In Question 183 we saw 1 c4 e6. Then 2 ♘c3 d5 can become a Queen's Gambit Declined after 3 d4 transposes into a more familiar order.

There are many routes to the same opening position. For example, 1 e4 e5 2 ♘f3 ♘c6 3 ♘c3 ♘f6 is the most common way of entering the Four Knights Game.

But it can also arise, quite logically, after 2 ♘c3 ♘c6 3 ♘f3 and then 3...♘f6. Also 2 ♘f3 ♘f6 3 ♘c3 and now 3...♘c6.

191. There seems to be a lot I could learn about the opening I choose. What do I really need to know?

You need to know the traps to avoid and what the main lines and common transpositions are.

Let's go back to the King's Gambit, **1 e4 e5 2 f4**. You need to know that 2...d5 sets a trap – 3 fxe5?? loses to 3...♛h4+.

You should know 3 exd5 e4 leads to a valid opening, called the Falkbeer Countergambit. But you should also know that 3...exf4 transposes into a main line of the King's Gambit.

Then, you need to know what that main line looks like. It normally arises after **1 e4 e5 2 f4 exf4** and then **3 ♘f3**.

One of the popular responses is **3...d5** and then **4 exd5 ♘f6**.

White to move

Because this occurs often, you should learn what to do now by looking up your options. They begin with 5 ♗c4 and 5 ♗b5+.

This opening is not likely to get you an advantage against a good opponent. But you can play it without having to memorize another ten moves of "book."

192. Are there openings that require knowing very few book moves?

Yes, in fact there are a few that you can play virtually without looking at your opponent's moves.

You can do this by keeping your pieces and pawns on your first three ranks. This delays a confrontation with your opponent's pieces and pawns for half a dozen moves at least.

For instance, Black can start with ...g6 and ...♗g7, as well as ...b6 and ...♗b7 and along with ...e6 and ...d6. He develops his knights at e7 and d7.

This is very conservative. But Boris Spassky used it in a world championship match and drew.

193. Can White do anything like that?

Sure. One option is 1 ♘f3 followed by 2 b3, 3 ♗b2, 4 e3 and 5 ♗e2.

Another is 1 f4 followed by 2 ♘f3, 3 e3, 4 ♗e2 and 5 0-0. This is a version of Bird's Opening.

These openings are not popular with masters because they offer little chance for White to get an advantage. But they are popular with non-masters because they are easy to remember.

There is also a White opening that begins 1 ♘f3 followed by 2 g3, 3 ♗g2, 4 0-0 and 5 d3. This is called the King's Indian Reversed.

Bird's Opening

194. Why "Reversed"?

Some opening schemes of Black can be used by White, and vice versa.

The King's Indian Reversed is nearly a mirror image of the King's Indian Defense. This usually begins 1 d4 ♘f6 and continues with 2...g6, 3...♗g7 followed in some order by ...d6 and ...0-0. Both openings feature a fianchettoed king bishop.

195. Why do the openings have so many foreign words, like fianchetto?

Many of the opening names and common moves were studied in Italy and other countries when they were chess centers, in the 16th to 18th centuries.

"Fianchetto" just means developing a bishop on one of two "long diagonals," a1-h8 and h1-a8. You can show off by pronouncing it correctly, "fee-an-KEH-to," not "fyan-chet-to."

There is also Giuoco Piano ("Quiet Game") and many hard-to-pronounce openings named after players and locations. Even the word "gambit" is foreign. It means to offer material, such as a pawn sacrifice, but comes from an Italian expression to describe tripping an opponent.

196. What if I just imitate White's moves when I'm Black? If he plays 1 e4, I play 1...e5 and so on.

This works well – until he makes a move you cannot imitate.

This can happen very quickly. For example, **1 e4 e5 2 ♘f3 ♘f6 3 ♘xe5 ♘xe4 4 ♕e2**.

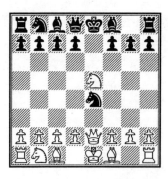

Black to move

And now **4...♕e7? 5 ♕xe4 ♕xe5?? 6.♕xe5+**. Or **4...♘f6 5 ♘c6+**.

It doesn't make sense that a player who moves second should be able to imitate his opponent indefinitely.

A similar version after 1 d4 would run **1...d5 2 c4 c5 3 cxd5 cxd4? 4 ♕xd4 ♕xd5?? 5 ♕xd5**.

197. I've seen the terms "open games," "closed games" and "semi-open games." What are they?

These are terms for three general classes of openings.

Open games begin 1 e4 e5. In semi-open games Black replies to 1 e4 in some other way. Closed games begin 1 d4 and other non-1 e4 moves.

The names are obsolete and misleading. They have little to do with whether the center is open or closed.

198. What are the practical differences between 1 e4 and 1 d4?

Games that begin 1 e4 tend to be more tactical and require more memory to play and more calculating ability to play well.

Two centuries ago there was virtually no analysis of 1 d4. But there was "book" analysis that ran more than 15 moves of openings such as the Muzio Gambit, **1 e4 e5 2 f4 exf4 3 ♘f3 g5 4 ♗c4 g4 5 0-0 gxf3 6 ♕xf3**.

Other openings have somewhat less piece-to-piece contact. "When you play 1 d4 you are sometimes able to play the opening using only common sense," Grandmaster Viktor Korchnoi said.

Nigel Short, another world-class player, said players "of my advanced age should be forbidden from playing 1 e4 for health reasons." And he was 45 at the time.

199. Why is it considered wrong to develop the queen early in the game?

It violates the principle of preserving options as well as another rule that can be summed up as "strongest last."

That is, the strongest pieces should be the last pieces to move for the first time. They are likely to be attacked by minor pieces if they advance past the second rank.

Grandmaster Yasser Seirawan said he learned this the hard way. He began his chess career by opening games with 1 h4 d5 2 ♖h3?? ♗xh3.

He followed this with a2-a4 and ♖a3, allowing ...♗xa3. "My rooks were never around for very long," he recalled.

200. Then why do masters move the queen early in some games?

For tactical reasons. Tactics usually trump everything else.

Consider the ancient opening that begins **1 e4 e5 2 f4 exf4 3 ♘c3 ♕h4+ 4 ♔e2**. Garry Kasparov revived this in a St. Louis blitz tournament in 2017.

The queen check was considered dubious. Previously, White had obtained reasonable chances after 4...d6, 4...c6, 4...♘c6, 4...♘e7 and 4...d5 5 ♘xd5 ♗g4+.

But Kasparov's opponent, Sergey Karjakin, chose **4...♕d8!**.

White to move

Black has lost two tempi (see Question 147). This is the same position as after 3 ♘c3 but with White to move and with the addition of ♔e2.

Yet Black is better because White has lost the right to castle. Getting his king to safety will take some time better spent on development. Kasparov managed to swindle Black out of a win.

201. Why is kingside castling more common than queenside castling?

It is usually faster, because you typically bring out both your KB and KN ahead of your QB and QN as well as your queen.

Queenside castling also requires you to guard more squares near your king. The a-pawn is often unprotected after 0-0-0.

On the other hand, after 0-0-0 the d1-rook is more likely to be immediately useful than the f1-rook after 0-0.

202. Why is BxN played in so many openings?

There are several reasons and **1 e4 e5 2 ♘f3 ♘c6 3 ♗b5 a6 4 ♗xc6 dxc6** illustrates a few.

White to move

Black's c-pawns are doubled and that compensates White for the absence of his bishop. Also, 4 ♗xc6 gains time compared with 4 ♗a4. White is ahead in development after **5 0-0.**

In addition, knights are generally better than bishops when there are so many pawns on the board to restrict the range of bishops. (See Question 24.)

The early superiority of knights is one of many reasons the opening is different from the later stages of the game.

203. Are there other differences I should know?

Yes, in the opening, pieces are less likely to protect one another.

Double attacks are more common. Until the kings are castled, the chances for tactics based on checks and mates are much higher than in the middlegame.

204. What do I do if my opponent plays an opening move I don't know?

What do you mean "if"?

There comes a point in every game when your opponent will play a move you don't know. Until you are a master, that point will probably occur in the opening.

José Capablanca offered a rule a century ago. It is a huge over-simplification but still has some benefit:

When you face an unfamiliar enemy move you should develop your remaining pieces, place them on protected squares and safeguard your king.

205. Any advice for which opening books I should read?

There are too many good books to mention. But there are telltale signs of a bad opening book:

It is biased. Don't trust a book that claims "1 h4! wins."

It is outdated. When you flip through it, you don't see any games played in the last three years.

It ignores transpositions.

It is an ego trip. Many of the games cited were played by the author.

206. I see a lot of terms in books I don't understand. What is a countergambit?

It's an obsolete term that used to mean an opening that meets a gambit with a counter-offer of a pawn.

The openings that actually deserve that name are the Falkbeer Countergambit (**1 e4 e5 2 f4 d5 3 exd5 e4**) and the Albin Countergambit (**1 d4 d5 2 c4 e5 3 dxe5 d4**). Nowadays, countergambit means just about any pawn offer by Black.

207. What is a tabiya?

Another foreign word, from Sanskrit, no less. Masters use it to describe a position that serves as a fork in the road of a major opening.

It typically comes when standard opening moves end and the players have to choose a middlegame strategy.

For example, **1 d4 d5 2 c4 e6 3 ♘c3 ♘f6 4 ♘f3 c5 5 cxd5 ♘xd5 6 e4 ♘xc3 7 bxc3 cxd4 8 cxd4 ♗b4+ 9 ♗d2 ♗xd2+ 10 ♕xd2 0-0.**

White to move

Masters often blitz the first ten moves and begin to think here.

White can play in the center with **11 ♗c4**, with the idea of d4-d5. Or he can take aim at one of the wings after 11 ♗d3 or 11 ♗e2.

The term tabiya comes from the precursor of modern chess, a much slower-paced game. Instead of quickly seizing central squares, the two players typically spent their first dozen moves marshalling their pieces behind a shield of pawns. There were several ways of doing this, each called a tabiya. (See Question 425 for an example.)

This is a sophisticated concept and you won't need to know it until you are strong enough to care about finding the best moves in a tabiya. Before that you may be interested in developing a repertoire.

208. What is a repertoire?

It is the package of all the openings you feel comfortable playing.

Some players like to have a repertoire built upon common themes. For example, as Black they play ...d5 and ...c6, in that order or reversed, on the first two moves of a game.

In that way, they reach middlegames with similar pawn structures after 1 e4 c6 2 d4 d5 3 ♘c3 dxe4 4 ♘xe4 or 1 d4 d5 2 c4 c6 3 ♘f3 ♘f6 4 ♘c3 dxc4 and later ♗xc4.

209. Why don't grandmasters play the same openings as everyone else?

You might ask, "Why don't amateurs play the same openings as grandmasters?"

You can probably answer that yourself:

Amateurs like openings that are easy to play, such as the Morra Gambit (**1 e4 c5 2 d4 cxd4 3 c3**). Masters play openings they can devote many hours to study.

Also, gambits are fun to play. You don't have to work hard to obtain an initiative, and your opponent may not know the lines that test them most.

Examples include the Blackmar-Diemer Gambit (**1 d4 d5 2 e4**), the Göring Gambit (**1 e4 e5 2 ♘f3 ♘c6 3 d4 exd4 4 c3**) and Belgrade Gambit (**1 e4 e5 2 ♘f3 ♘c6 3 ♘c3 ♘f6 4 d4 exd4 5 ♘d5**).

No grandmaster would play the Danish Gambit (**1 e4 e5 2 d4 exd4 3 c3 dxc3 4 ♗c4 cxb2 5 ♗xb2**) in a game that mattered.

Black to move

The reason is there is book analysis that shows how Black can easily achieve equal chances. But at the amateur level it is a fine opening.

Aside from gambits, there are openings favored by many amateurs because they are low-maintenance.

210. What do you mean by maintenance?

The amount of study you need to play an opening in competition. Maintenance keeps your opening knowledge up to date.

High-maintenance openings are trendy. New moves change the "theory" periodically in the Najdorf Variation and Dragon Variation of the Sicilian Defense, for instance.

Low-maintenance openings don't take much to learn and their theory changes slowly. Once you know these openings you don't have to keep up on what the latest grandmaster games have to say about them.

Among the lower-maintenance openings for Black are the Sicilian variation that begins **1 e4 c5 2 ♘f3 ♘c6 3 d4 cxd4 4 ♘xd4 ♛b6** and the Bogo-Indian Defense (**1 d4 ♘f6 2 c4 e6 3 ♘f3 ♗b4+**).

For White, the French Defense line that runs **1 e4 e6 2 d4 d5 3 exd5 exd5 3 c4** and the Colle System are low-maintenance.

211. What if books describe the opening I want to play as bad?

Then you want to know two things: How bad? And how well-known is the opening?

Frank Marshall, the longest-reigning US champion, played his favorite variation of the French Defense, **1 e4 e6 2 d4 d5 3 ♘c3** and now **3...c5**. He scored well against masters.

Theory says White has clearly the better chances, after **4 exd5 exd5 5 dxc5 ♘f6 6 ♗e3 ♘c6**.

White to move

The Marshall Variation has disappeared from almost all opening books. However, only one player out of a hundred knows the book moves.

212. Why does Black shut in his bishop with 1...e6 in the French?

He wants to block the best diagonal, ♗c4-f7, of White's bishop with 2...d5.

Many major openings require a slight concession by Black. For instance, in the Caro-Kann Defense, 1 e4 c6, his pawn occupies the best square for his b8-knight.

Black usually trades a bishop for a knight in the Winawer Variation of the French Defense (**1 e4 e6 2 d4 d5 3 ♘c3 ♗b4**) and many lines of the Nimzo-Indian Defense (**1 d4 ♘f6 2 c4 e6 3 ♘c3 ♗b4**).

He loses time with his queen in the Center Counter Defense (**1 e4 d5 2 exd5 ♕xd5 3 ♘c3**).

But these are legitimate openings with excellent chances for Black to equalize.

213. What do you mean by "to equalize"?

To achieve winning chances as great as your opponent. This term is often used in the late opening to denote when White no longer enjoys the advantage he got after making the game's first move.

Some players, when they have Black, seek to equalize. Others play for sharper positions in which the chances for a major advantage are much greater.

The choice is a question of how ambitious you are. Lajos Portisch was an expert on openings but took a modest view. "Your only task in the opening is to reach a playable middlegame," he said.

214. This seems like a lot to memorize. Is it?

Masters like to say, "Don't memorize openings. It is much more important to understand the ideas behind them." But that goes only so far.

Some things have to be memorized. If I asked you, "What is six times seven?" would you use "understanding" to get the right answer? Or would you rely on the multiplication table you memorized as a kid?

215. Once I've learned about 1 e4 e5, how should I pick additional openings to play and study?

The main factors are your temperament, ambitions and memory: Do you like sharp middlegames or quiet ones? Do you feel you need an edge as White or just a playable position? Is a solid middlegame your main goal or is counterplay?

A good way to learn a new opening is to adopt a hero (Question 117).

There are databases you can easily search to find, for example, more than 600 games of Vishy Anand's that begin with the Ruy Lopez. Or search for Akiba Rubinstein in the Queen's Gambit Declined.

For more complex openings, search for David Bronstein's King's Indian Defense games or Bobby Fischer's Najdorf Variation wins.

216. Should I learn a lot about a few openings or a little about several?

This is the old "breadth or depth?" question. Some players, like Fischer, liked to know a lot about two or three favorite systems. Magnus Carlsen is the opposite.

But until you are stronger, go with depth. Better to know the first eight moves of a defense to 1 e4 than the first four moves of five defenses to it.

The most important advice is simple: Choose an opening you feel at ease with. "If you don't play what you like and you are never comfortable with it, you will never be able to play it well," said GM Walter Browne.

Chapter Ten: Pawns

217. Why do masters make a big deal about pawn structures?

Because structures last so long and influence the pieces so much.

After the first dozen or so moves, pawns typically form a distinct pattern. Thirty moves later, almost all of the first-rank pieces will probably have been captured. But much of the pawn structure may remain.

In the middlegame, the structure shows you where to put your rooks, bishops and knights. A favorable structure makes an attack much more likely to succeed.

Kasparov – Short

London 1993

Black to move

A pawn at e5 often benefits a White attack because Black cannot defend his kingside with, for example, a knight on f6.

Black had just played ...♘c7. If he continued with 19...♘a6 and ...♘b4, White could grow his advantage with 20 ♖xc8 ♗xc8 21 ♖c1 and ♕c2, attacking h7.

Or 20...♗xc8 21 ♕xb6 and ♖c1.

Instead, Black chose **19...♗b4?** and lost after **20 ♗xh7+! ♔xh7 21 ♘g5+! ♔g8 22 ♖h3 ♖e8 23 ♕f3 ♕d7 24 ♕h5 ♔f8 25 ♘h7+ ♔e7 26 ♗g5+ f6 27 ♘xf6 resigns.**

218. Are all pawns equal in value?

Equal in exchange value. But pawns vary widely in their usefulness and liabilities during a game, more so than that of first-rank pieces.

In that way, a pawn can be worth much more than a pawn near it.

219. What does that depend on?

On the file a pawn occupies, how far it is advanced and how it relates to fellow pawns.

Pawns closest to the center are most valuable because they improve control of key squares. There was a time when authorities such as Emanuel Lasker and Rudolf Spielmann said that a bishop pawn or knight pawn was worth only a fraction of a central pawn. And the rook pawns are a special case.

220. Why?

Because a rook pawn can only capture in one direction, inward. All other pawns can capture in two directions, to their left or right.

Lasker said at the beginning of the game a rook pawn is worth a quarter of a central pawn. This is an extreme view that no one shares today. Computers that analyzed gazillions of games found that a rook pawn is worth 80 to 85 percent of another pawn.

221. What does that mean for me?

You may have a choice of which pawn to make a capture. The best policy is to capture towards the center, and this is especially true for a rook pawn.

1 d4 ♘f6 2 c4 e6 3 ♘f3 b6 4 ♘c3 ♗b7 5 ♗g5 ♗b4 6 ♖c1 h6 7 ♗h4 g5 8 ♗g3 ♘h5 9 e3 ♘xg3

White to move

You may be tempted by 10 fxg3. Then White may have better chances of exploiting the half-open f-file than he would of making use of the h-file after 10 hxg3.

But experience confirms the capture-towards-the-center rule. White is worse after 10 fxg3? g4 11 ♘h4 ♛g5!.

222. How else does a pawn's value change?

By advancing. This is obvious today. But before the 20th century many masters believed pawns should not move past the fourth rank unless they had good chances of queening.

Their reasoning was that a pawn on d3 or d4 has more influence on the center than one on d5, as Steinitz said in his influential book *The Modern Chess Instructor*.

But Steinitz changed his mind. He later endorsed openings such as 1 e4 e6 2 e5 because of the way the e-pawn restricts Black's pieces.

Today the master consensus says a protected pawn tends to gain in value as it advances. One theory holds that a protected pawn on the sixth rank is twice as valuable as it was on the third or fourth rank.

223. How can I use this information?

It can make your evaluation of a position more accurate. For example, who do you think stands better in this position?

Van Foreest – Grandelius

Wijk aan Zee 2021

White to move

You might conclude Black has at least equal chances because the most significant pawns are the ones at d6 and e6.

They can favorably influence the center by advancing, for example with 21...e5!. Or after 21 ♕b3 d5! (22 cxd5 ♘xd5 23 ♗xd5 exd5 24 ♕xd5 ♖d8!).

But this evaluation changes after **21 ♘b5! axb5 22 cxb5.**

White's two passed pawns on the fifth rank threaten to advance.

For example, 22...e5 23 b6! ♗f5 24 ♕b5 ♗xb1 25 ♖xb1 is strong, even a rook down.

Black returned the knight sacrifice, **22...♗xb5 23 ♕xb5 ♘d7 24 ♗b7 ♕d8 25 a6**, but eventually lost.

224. What about the third criterion you mentioned, how a pawn relates to other pawns?

This is usually the most important way of evaluating pawns. The priority list starts with passed pawns. We saw the power of the passed a- and b-pawns in the last example.

In an endgame, a passed pawn is royalty. It is (not yet) a queen. But it can demand the respect of a princess.

White to move

After **1 b4 cxb4 2 cxb4,** the b4-pawn is more than just passed. It is an "outside" passed pawn because it is has a clear path to queening.

If Black plays **1...c4** instead of 1...cxb4, White's b-pawn becomes even more valuable as a "protected passed pawn." White wins more easily than after 1...cxb4.

A protected passed pawn is normally sufficient to win a king and pawn ending and is a big advantage in other endgames.

225. Which pawns are considered disadvantageous?

Isolated, backward and doubled pawns.

They are inferior because of two qualities – their vulnerability and their difficulty in creating a passed pawn.

White to move

An isolated pawn, like the one at a2, is vulnerable in a middlegame because it is separated by at least one file from other White pawns and cannot be defended by them.

White's c-pawns are doubled. They may be easier to defend in a middlegame than isolated pawns. But it is problematic to create a passed pawn out of them in an endgame.

The g2-pawn is backward because it cannot advance without allowing the Black h-pawn to capture it.

The Black f-pawns are the weakest because they are doubled and isolated.

226. Are the f-pawns also inferior because of the squares they guard?

Not necessarily. They control four squares. If they stood abreast at f6 and g6 they would also control four.

The main reasons the pawns would be more valuable on f6 and g6 is that they are better able to create a passed pawn and less vulnerable to attack from, for example, a rook.

In the middlegame, the vulnerability of a pawn counts more. In an endgame, the queenability counts more.

227. How much better are connected pawns than isolated pawns in an endgame?

Often whether the pawns are connected is the difference between an easy win and a doubtful one.

White to move

This kind of position can be won by White without great effort. It won't happen quickly. If both sides make the best moves, Black should last no more than 30 moves.

But if we could somehow shift the White g-pawn to h2, it suddenly becomes a drawable ending because it is easier for Black to blockade the pawns. Several world-class players have failed to win very similar positions with the White pieces.

228. Are there any benefits to having unhealthy pawns?

Yes. A backward pawn often supports a strong center pawn.

Backward Pawns

Black's d- and b-pawns are backward.

They create holes at b5 and d5 that White can occupy with pieces and not be threatened by a pawn.

But there is a benefit to the e5-pawn. If it were on e6, the weakness of the d6-pawn would largely disappear. But White might put a piece safely – and strongly – on d4 or f4.

One of the major opening discoveries of the past century was the realization that Black can afford a backward d6-pawn in the Sicilian Defense.

When a game begins **1 e4 c5 2 ♘f3 d6 3 d4 cxd4 4 ♘xd4**, White has traded off a center pawn but in compensation he obtained a fine square for his knight at d4.

However, after **4...♘f6 5 ♘c3**, both **5...♘c6 6 ♗e2 e5** and **5...a6 6 ♗e2 e5** are considered sound openings because they deny White that square. The weakness of Black's d6-pawn is difficult to exploit.

229. What about isolated pawns?

An isolated passed pawn can suddenly become a powerful asset if a rook is behind it, pushing it forward. It can look like a weakling on the second rank but a tower of strength on the fifth or sixth.

An isolated d-pawn, an "isolani" as it is called, can be very useful in the middlegame. On d4, a White pawn can support a knight, on e5 or c5. This is a benefit that diminishes as other pieces are traded.

There is a famous Siegbert Tarrasch quote: "The isolated d-pawn may prove a weakness in the endgame. But before the endgame the gods have placed the middlegame."

230. I've heard the term "artificially isolated" pawn. What does that mean?

It means a pawn that is not separated by a file from its brother pawns but can no longer be protected by them.

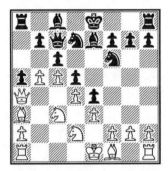

Kasparov – Fritz X3D

New York 2003

White to move

Now **12 b6!** ensures that the a5-pawn cannot be defended by Black's b-pawn. It is artificially isolated.

White can capture it without much interference and was winning after ♘b3xa5.

231. Is there any way doubled pawns are good?

They lose some of their ability to queen but retain the ability to stop enemy pawns from queening.

White to move

White cannot create a passed pawn with just pawn moves.

For instance, 1 f5 gxf5 2 gxf5 would succeed if he could continue 3 h5 and 4 h6!.

But Black can stop that with …h6.

In the middlegame, the capture that creates doubled pawns can be beneficial because it opens at least half of a file.

For example, a Petroff Defense line runs **1 e4 e5 2 ♘f3 ♘f6 3 ♘xe5 d6 4 ♘f3 ♘xe4 5 ♘c3 ♘xc3 6 dxc3**. Chances are considered balanced because of White's play from a rook on the d-file.

But this compensation disappears by the endgame.

If there are no rooks on the board, a doubled pawn is only worth 5/8th of an undoubled pawn, according to a computer analysis by Grandmaster Larry Kaufman.

That's pretty esoteric information. More useful is knowing that there may be opportunities to undouble pawns.

232. How can you undouble pawns?

The same way that you change the file of any pawn, by a capture.

Wilhelm Steinitz criticized Paul Morphy for failing to appreciate this in his most famous game. It began **1 e4 e5 2 ♘f3 d6 3 d4 ♗g4 4 dxe5 ♗xf3**.

White to move

Morphy won after **5 ♕xf3**. Steinitz said 5 gxf3 was better because of 5…dxe5 6 ♕xd8+ ♔xd8 7 f4!.

This will be followed by an exchange of the f4-pawn for the e5-pawn. Then White will have the better chances because of his two-bishop advantage and nice pawn structure.

233. *Are there connected pawns that are bad to have in the middlegame?*

There are some configurations of them that can be bad *or* good. One is the hanging pawns.

Hanging pawns

Hanging pawns are two connected pawns that are not passed but have no pawn on a file in front of them. The version in the diagram is common in many middlegames that derive from 1 d4.

They are subject to attack from Black's heavy pieces on the c- and d-files. But they give White an advantage in central space and the opportunity to create a passed pawn with d4-d5.

The "hangers" are strongest when the pawns stand abreast. If the c-pawn is at c3, not c4, Black might get the upper hand by establishing a blockade with pieces on c4 and d5. The c4 square can be an ideal outpost for a knight.

234. *What is an outpost?*

One player's pawn hole is his opponent's potential outpost.

Black's move in the next diagram is a positional blunder because it hands White an outpost square.

Nimzovich – Levenfish

Carlsbad 1911

Black to move

Black recaptured **9...♘xf6?**.

He was worse after **10 ♘e5 ♗d6 11 dxc5 ♗xc5 12 ♗g5** and eventually lost.

Black knew that 9...gxf6! was positionally correct. But he had an unfounded fear of 10 ♘e5 – 10...fxe5 11 ♕h5+ ♔e7! is quite safe.

235. OK, what do I really need to know about pawn structures?

Early in your career you need to have a general idea of what good and bad structures look like.

To improve beyond that you need to know how to exploit a good structure.

Kasparov – Piket
Zurich 2001

1 e4 c5 2 ♘f3 ♘c6 3 ♘c3 e5 4 ♗c4 ♗e7 5 d3 d6 6 ♘d2 ♘f6 7 ♘f1 ♘a5 8 ♘e3 ♘xc4 9 dxc4!

Black to move

White accepted doubled c-pawns rather than 9 ♘xc4 because he wanted to prevent Black from obtaining play with ...d5 or ...b5.

Once White recognizes that the dxc4 structure is favorable he can exploit the closed center.

Garry Kasparov developed a winning kingside attack after **9...0-0 10 ♕f3 g6 11 g4 ♗e6 12 h4 ♕d7 13 ♖g1**.

236. In the total scheme of things, how important are pawn moves?

"Nothing compromises a position like pawn moves," Tarrasch said. A pawn move can't be taken back.

Pawn moves are also limited. Every first-rank piece has an almost infinite number of possibilities in the course of a long game. But no pawn can make more than six moves.

As another great player put it, if you never push a pawn, you will never make a mistake.

That said, pawn play and the many different pawn structures should be part of your chess education *after* you are comfortable with piece play. The more important topics on the path to becoming a good player are the ones we've looked at so far – tactics, material values, trading and the like.

Next on our agenda is putting these principles and techniques to work with the help of calculation. This is one aspect of choosing a move that has become more important in the 21st century.

Chapter Eleven: Calculating

237. How far ahead do average players see before they make a move?

Two moves is more than most players can see.

Three moves is about the maximum for serious tournament players.

238. But masters must calculate much further?

Yes, when they believe they need to calculate. But they make most of their moves without that much look-ahead.

Even elite players are not calculating machines. "Normally I would calculate three to five moves," Garry Kasparov said. "You don't need more."

239. Aren't there positions in which they look 10 moves into the future?

Yes, but as Bent Larsen put it, "A position has to be very simple if you can just calculate."

Grandelius – Donchenko

Wijk aan Zee 2021

White to move

Black resigned after **47 ♚g5!**.

Annotators pointed out a probable continuation: 47...♚e4 48 ♚f6! ♚xf4 49 ♚xe6 ♚e4 50 ♚d6.

Then would come 50... ♚d3 51 ♚c7 ♚xc3 52 ♚xb7 ♚xb4 53 ♚xc6, and White queens in at most five moves.

The reason masters can calculate an 11-move sequence like this is the *evaluation part of calculating* is elementary. This is what Larsen meant by "very simple."

At each point in that sequence the position can be accurately judged by asking the question "Who queens first?"

240. But White still had to see 11 moves ahead. Isn't that super-difficult?

Not really. There were no possible positions in that sequence in which you could say, "White is better. But it is not clear if he has enough to win."

All White had to see was that if he can promote at least one move before Black, he wins.

It is actually more difficult to look three moves ahead when you have to evaluate several complex positions that could arise after the first two moves.

241. How much stronger will I be if I can calculate one full move more than I do now?

A lot. A good guess would be more than 300 rating points, a huge amount. We learned this from research on early chess-playing computers.

In computer lingo, a "ply" is half of a full move.

Some of the first engines could calculate three-ply deep. In the last diagram, this means considering 47 ♔g5, Black's response 47...♔e4 and then 48 ♔f6.

They couldn't accurately calculate further than that. But this allowed them to play at about 1100 strength.

When a computer was improved so it could see five ply, it reached 1500. This level is better than about two thirds of U.S. tournament players

A computer that could see seven ply jumped to a rating of more than 2000, putting it in the top 3 percent.

But bear in mind, grandmasters generally calculate *less* than mere masters.

242. How is that possible?

They consider fewer candidate moves.

They don't waste time on candidates that are unlikely to be good. Their intuition tells them which moves are worthy of a deeper look.

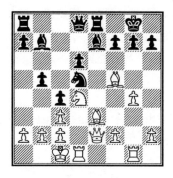

Caruana – Duda

Wijk aan Zee 2021

White to move

Black has just played 15...♘d5 and prepared to capture on e3.

Most players would try to weigh how dangerous 16...♘xe3 really is. They would consider White moves that allowed it, such as 16 g5.

But a master would know that Black stands better if he gets to play 16...♘xe3!.

He would focus on moves that prevent the capture, such as 16 ♗d2, or might discourage it, such as with 16 ♕f3. He thinks more efficiently than non-masters.

A grandmaster is even more efficient. He would quickly determine that only two candidate moves were worth calculating.

One is 16 ♗e4. The other is the forcing 16 ♘e6.

243. And that's the secret to grandmaster calculation?

No. A grandmaster can calculate a candidate move further than other players when he wants to. The secret is that he knows when it is worth doing that.

In the last example, he might look at 16 ♗e4 and the forcing reply 16...♘xe3 17 ♗xb7 ♘xd1.

White to move

He would see that Black threatens 18...♗g5+ and ...♖xe2.

He might examine 18 ♔xd1 ♗f6 19 ♕f3 and see that 19...♗xd4 eliminates the possibility of ♘c6.

He would not give up on the variation until he looks at 20 ♗xa8.

But once he sees 20...♗xf2!, a desperado, and calculates its consequences, he would suspect 16 ♗e4? leads to a bad position.

In the tree of variations, this was one of the few very long branches.

244. What do you mean "tree"?

"Tree of variations" is a term masters use to describe what a player should analyze when it is his turn to move.

Imagine a large tree. Each branch begins with a candidate move and extends out. The length of a branch depends on the number of moves that stem from it.

To select your next move you should evaluate the positions at the end of each branch. Then compare them.

In the last example, White evaluated a few branches, including one that begins **16 ♘e6!**. It led to the most favorable position at its end. He played it and nearly won.

In practice, masters don't always follow the "tree" method. Their thought processes are more chaotic and influenced by their intuition and other factors.

As Grandmaster Anatoly Lein put it, "I don't think like a tree. Do you think like a tree?"

245. Are there positions even grandmasters cannot calculate accurately?

Of course. There are often complex positions in which there are too many branches to look at. Or the ends of the branches are too complex to evaluate definitively.

Calculation only gives them a general sense of their possibilities. They base their choice of move on that sense.

The same yardstick can be used by average players. Like grandmasters, they can make an educated guess. The difference is that the GMs have more data on which to base their guess.

246. There are so many different moves to consider in each position. How does a master trim the list?

He looks first at forcing moves. Checks, captures and moves that make threats are the most likely tree branches.

A famous example of failing to calculate forcing moves was:

Hübner – Petrosian

Biel 1976

White to move

If this were a "White to play and win" quiz position, experienced players would look for checks.

They would quickly see that 37 ♕e8+ wins. The rest is 37...♔g7 38 ♖e7+ ♔h6 39 ♕f8+ ♔h5 40 ♖xh7 mate.

There are very few branches and none that requires much evaluation. For example, 38...♔f6 is mated by 39 ♕f7.

But in the game White played **37 g3??** and lost.

247. When can I stop calculating a move? Is it after I see two moves ahead? After three?

You can stop when there are no significant replies by your opponent.

In the last example, once White sees 37 ♕e8+, he would continue until he was stopped by 40 ♖xh7 mate. Clearly, there is nothing more to look at.

Computer programmers gave us a word for something we already knew, "quiescence." It essentially means when you reach a point in a calculated sequence when there are no "loud" moves to consider.

Take the example of **1 e4 e5 2 ♘f3 ♘c6 3 ♗b5 a6 4 ♗xc6 dxc6 5 d4 exd4 6 ♕xd4**:

Black to move

Only a very bad calculator would look at **6...♕xd4** and conclude, "Black is winning. He is a queen ahead. No reason to calculate further."

Of course, there is. After **7 ♘xd4,** material is equal. There are still forcing moves to consider, such as 7...c5 and 7...♝c5. But the position is fairly quiet.

248. What are the most common mistakes I can make when I calculate?

We already talked about making a faulty assumption (Question 90). A more fundamental error is to misevaluate the end of a tree branch.

Capablanca – Alekhine

Nottingham 1936

Black to move

In this notorious example, Black thought he was winning material with **24...f4 25 gxf4 ♝f5.**

He had calculated four moves beyond that, **26 ♕d2 ♝xd3 27 exd3 c5 28 ♖xc3 ♝xc3 29 ♕xc3.**

That part was accurate. But he had mentally miscounted the pieces.

He thought he had given up two minor pieces for two rooks. In other words, he had won two Exchanges.

But he had actually given up three minor pieces. That's not nearly enough and he lost.

249. How can I train myself to calculate better?

There is a simple method that will not seem like studying: Pick up a chess book or magazine and look at an annotated game. There will probably be a diagram after every few moves.

Look at one diagram and cover the next diagram in the game. Then think about the moves played after the first diagram. Try to visualize them. You are performing an elementary form of calculation.

Then uncover the second diagram. If it depicts what you visualized, your calculation was correct.

Tigran Petrosian said he did this with every book or chess magazine he found when he was ten. By 13 he was not only able to calculate relatively long variations but to play blindfold chess.

250. But I'm never going to play blindfold chess, am I?

When you calculate, you are playing a kind of blindfold chess. You probably have a good "blind" sense of the board already.

Here's a test: Close your eyes. Imagine a board that is empty except for a White bishop on a1. You should be able to mentally see how the bishop can move to h8.

Now, imagine the bishop getting there one move at a time. What is the first move? You should be able to visualize that the next square is b2. The move would be ♗b2.

What is the next square? The one after that?

After testing yourself in similar ways, with a friend, you should be able to tell – with your eyes closed – the color of each square on the board.

Is c7 a white square or a black one? What about g5? And d3?

This develops a mental feeling for the board. For reasons we don't know, masters develop this feeling. Many masters can play blindfold chess, without knowing it.

251. I look at games on a computer, rather than books and magazines. What should I do to improve my calculation?

It is even easier with a computer. Choose a game you want to look at on a site with a database, such as chessgames.com.

Stop at some point after the opening. Take a good look at the diagram. Then read the text that shows the next one or two full moves.

Try to visualize what that would look like. Check yourself by clicking on those moves. Do this throughout the game. Gradually you can build this up, from one or two moves to three or four or more.

If you work really hard on this, you may be able to play through an entire game in your head. This is excellent calculation training. And, who knows, you might be able to play a "blind" game with a friend

252. Is there a proper attitude to becoming a good calculator?

Yes. Trust yourself, not your opponent.

If he makes a move you foresaw – but considered bad – don't assume you were wrong.

Maybe he saw something further that you didn't. But maybe his move is simply bad. Recheck your analysis to make sure.

As we'll see in the next few chapters, being able to calculate better is valuable in making sound sacrifices. It is even more important when you are defending than when you are attacking. And it may make up for a lack of knowledge of some basic endgame positions and of techniques for winning a won game.

Chapter Twelve: Sacrificing

253. *Why does a sacrifice make sense? It means you have less material to attack with.*

But not at the area of the board you are attacking.

Compare it with war: A more skillful army may win when it concentrates its forces at an area where a larger army is spread thin.

By giving up some of his material, the sacrificer hopes to generate greater force at that point of attack. A sacrifice turns "matter into energy," as a great attacking player of the past, Rudolf Spielmann, put it.

254. *Are there different ways of doing that?*

Yes, and you may hear terms such as king-hunt sacrifice, decoy sacrifice, line-clearing sacrifice and so on. Like tactics (Question 62), the ideas behind these techniques are worth remembering, not necessarily the names.

Schlechter – Salwe

St. Petersburg 1909

White to move

In one of his books, Savielly Tartakower used the terms "irruptive sacrifice," "complementary sacrifice," among others. He called **30 ♖e6!** an "unmasking sacrifice."

What it unmasks is the queen's route to h6 (31 ♕xh6+ and 32 ♕g7 mate).

There was no way to protect h6 and Black resigned soon after **30...♖xe6 31 dxe6 d5 32 ♕xh6+ ♔e8 33 exf7+ ♔xf7 34 ♕h7+ ♔e6 35 ♕xg6**.

These terms are confusing because 30 ♖e6! is a sacrifice in name and appearance. But it is really what Spielmann called a "sham" sacrifice.

255. How so?

It carried no risk. The rook could not be accepted because Black would be mated after 30...fxe6??.

A "real" sacrifice is speculative, said Spielmann, in a classic book called *The Art of Sacrifice.* It is an educated guess that the risk will be rewarded.

Spielmann also drew a distinction between active and passive sacrifices.

256. How can a sacrifice be passive?

A sacrifice is often called an "offer" of material. A passive sacrifice can be safely declined – in fact, ignored.

Spielmann cited an ancient gambit: **1 e4 e5 2 f4 exf4 3 ♘f3 g5 4 h4 g4 5 ♘g5**.

Black to move

The knight has no safe retreat. Black can win it with 5...h6.

But he can ignore the knight, for example with 5...♘f6. White's offer was passive.

257. If I have a choice, is accepting a sacrifice better than declining?

Two world champions, Bobby Fischer and Mikhail Tal, took opposing views:

Fischer said you should accept if you can't find a good reason to refuse. He would agree with an old maxim: "It is better to sacrifice your opponent's pieces."

But Tal said the player who accepts is taking just as much of a risk as the sacrificer. Tal believed a sacrifice can be made if you can't find a good reason *not* to make it.

So, we don't have a clear answer to your question. But we have another maxim: "The only way to refute a sacrifice is to accept it."

In the last example, the sacrifice is unsound but only **5...h6!** proves this.

Then **6 ♘xf7** is an active sacrifice – active because it is a forcing move that forks Black's queen and rook. Black has little choice.

But **6...♔xf7** favors him because White's attack should soon sputter and die.

258. What material is most often sacrificed?

Pawns lead the list. Then comes the Exchange.

Anything greater than that is either very risky – or not risky at all. The rook sacrifice in Question 253 was a sham sacrifice.

A pawn or the Exchange are common offers because the risk is minor. Sacrificing them can be justified by relatively modest compensation.

259. What do you mean by compensation?

Compensation is a benefit, either material or positional, that may offset the risk of a sacrifice.

Getting a rook on the seventh rank in an endgame is an example of positional compensation for the loss of a pawn.

Compensation can be a mixture of material and positional benefits. There is a recurring theme in the Sicilian Defense when Black gives up a rook for a knight, ...♖xc3, and White retakes bxc3.

If Black then wins the pawn at c3, he nearly has material equality. He also has some positional compensation because White's other queenside pawns are damaged.

260. What is the typical compensation in an opening gambit?

A gain in time that results in better piece play and development.

The player who accepts a gambit pawn often has to delay his own development to keep the pawn. This is why there is little risk in the Queen's Gambit Accepted, **1 d4 d5 2 c4 dxc4**.

If Black tries to hold the extra pawn, **3 ♘f3 b5 4 a4 c6 5 e3 e6**, White can play **6 axb5 cxb5 7 b3!**.

Black to move

It is too much trouble for Black to try to hold his extra material. For example, **7...cxb3 8 ♗xb5+**.

261. What is the usual compensation for a minor piece?

There are two very different kinds. In one, the sacrificer tries to open up and exploit a target area, usually the enemy king position.

If you give up a knight for a pawn or two near an opponent's king, you have reduced your attacking force but also wiped out much of the defending force.

Jobava – Naiditsch

Wijk aan Zee 2006

White to move

There is no forced win after **22 ♘xg7!** if Black recaptures **22...♕xg7**. So, this is a real sacrifice, not a combination.

But after **23 ♗xh6 ♕f7** White can get a winning attack from 24 ♕g5+ and 25 ♗g6.

262. What is the other kind of minor piece sacrifice?

It happens when a player gives up a piece for pawns and hopes to win because of the power of his own pawns or other factors.

136

Wei Yi – Sadiku

Baku 2016

White to move

White's queenside pieces would be entombed after 11 ♘b1? b4!. But he could have safely played 11 ♘f1 and enjoyed a good middlegame.

He preferred **11 axb5!**. It is a "real" and forcing sacrifice (11....axb5?? 12 ♖xa8).

White got more than enough compensation after **11...cxd2 12 ♗xd2 ♘b8 13 bxa6**.

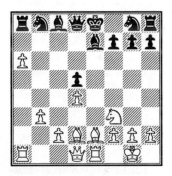

Black to move

Black's problems are illustrated by 13...♘f6 and then 14 ♗b5+ ♗d7 15 ♗a5! ♕c8 16 ♗b4 and a capture on e7.

The game ended with **13....♗xa6 14 ♗b5+ ♔f8 15 ♘e5 ♕d6 16 ♕h5 g6 17 ♗h6+ ♘xh6 18 ♕xh6+ ♔g8 19 ♗e8 resigns.**

263. Why do masters sacrifice the Exchange so often?

There are two reasons.

First, a rook is often much less useful than a minor piece in a middlegame. It grows in value as the game approaches an ending, as we saw in Question 25. The sacrificer expects that the impact of his compensation will be realized well before the endgame.

The second reason is that an Exchange sacrifice frequently comes with the compensation of an extra pawn. Then the material imbalance—minor piece plus pawn versus rook – is actually less than that of a pawn sacrifice. It is about half a pawn, the amount we talked about in Question 36.

264. Are there times when sacrifices are most likely to succeed?

In general, the greater the *total amount* of material on the board, the better the chances of success.

For example, sacrificing the Exchange carries more risk if it means giving up your last rook.

Also, if you want to sacrifice your queen for two minor pieces, you had better have at least three minor pieces of your own left to play with. Ideally, four.

When the total amount of material is reduced, by trades, true sacrifices are relatively rare. That is the case in endgames.

You will see endgame sacrifices that allow the sacrificer to queen a pawn. But that is another kind of sham sacrifice, a queening combination.

265. Is a sacrifice a form of tactic?

It can use many of the same themes as tactics. A sacrifice can be line-opening or line-closing, for example. Here is an example of how two crucial lines, a file and a diagonal, can be closed favorably.

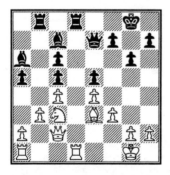

Liublinsky – Botvinnik

Moscow 1943

Black to move

White is preparing to win the c5-pawn after ♕f2 and ♘a4.

Black averted this by sealing the f2-c5 diagonal with **25...♖d4!**.

White could take the rook with his bishop, or with a knight after 26 ♘e2.

But a rook is worth a rook only when it can play like a rook. With the d-file closed, White's rooks were less effective than Black's minor pieces.

The value of this became clear after **26 ♘e2 ♝c8 27 ♘xd4 cxd4 28 ♝f2 c5 29 ♖f1 f5**.

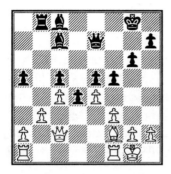

White to move

This confirms the point about total material on the board (Question 264). Black's sacrifice might not have been sound if a pair of rooks or the queens had been traded.

But with them on the board he seized the initiative and went on to win after **30 ♝g3 ♝d7 31 ♖ad1 f4 32 ♝f2 g5 33 g4 fxg3 34 ♝xg3 ♝h3 35 ♖f2 h5**.

266. Are there sacrifices that are essentially defensive?

Yes. And the last example was one.

Black ultimately won because of his kingside attack. But the primary goal of 25...♖d4 was to avoid the loss of the c5-pawn.

There are many other defensive sacrifices, with the goals of controlling a key square, blockading or eliminating a dangerous piece, and so on.

Black to move

White threatens to win material with 20 ♝g5. A natural defense is 19...♖d5 or 19...♖d7.

But **19...♖xd3** has been played. After 20 cxd3 ♕d7 and ...♕d5, Black obtains excellent play on light squares and good chances of winning one of the weak pawns, at a2, d3 or g2.

Black is worse but with good drawing chances after, for example, 21 ♗b4 ♕d5 22 ♔b1 ♘g6. Or 21 ♔b1 ♕xd3+ 22 ♔a1 ♘g6.

There is some irony in many sacrifices. Yes, the sacrificer's army is smaller in overall weight. But he has just as many pieces as his opponent – and more targets for his army to attack.

And getting back to Question 257, in some positions Mikhail Tal is right. The player who accepts a sacrifice is taking just as much risk as the player who makes the offer. And in some positions, Bobby Fischer is right about taking what is offered.

Chapter Thirteen: Endgames

267. When does the endgame start?

That's a simple question and there should be a simple answer. But we don't have one.

Among the definitions that have been suggested are:

a) When the kings can safely take part in play,

b) When neither player has more than the equivalent of a queen and a minor piece left, and

c) When the main goal of the players is promoting a pawn.

But one or more of these definitions fail to describe many positions we would definitely call endgames.

268. Isn't it always an endgame after the queens are traded?

Not if there is a lot of other material left on the board.

For instance, after **1 e4 d6 2 d4 e5 3 dxe5 dxe5 4 ♕xd8+ ♔xd8**.

White to move

None of the three definitions mentioned above apply. Neither player is thinking about queening a pawn. And while it is safer, it is not yet safe for the kings to take an active role.

Instead, the priorities of a middlegame are in force. After a typical continuation such as **5 ♗c4 f6 6 ♗e3 ♘d7 7 ♘c3 c6 8 0-0-0 ♔c7 9 f4!** White is trying to exploit Black's king position.

141

He can develop a winning initiative after minor errors by Black. This kind of position is often called, appropriately, a "queenless middlegame."

269. What should I do when the ending starts?

Think differently. Rid yourself of the middlegame thoughts you've embraced for the previous 20 or 30 moves.

You should evaluate each trade more carefully. With fewer pieces on the board, a favorable exchange might be enough to win. A poor exchange can lose.

Pawn trades are also different. In the middlegame, a player with the initiative may want to open lines by exchanging pawns. In the endgame, a trade of pawns usually helps the defense.

The endgame is so different that there is one way of thinking in the early endgame and a somewhat different mindset in the later stages.

270. How should I think differently in the late endgame?

You should calculate more.

This is surprising to many students. But it makes sense because there are fewer candidate moves to analyze.

Vachier-Lagrave – Carlsen

Internet 2021

White to move

There is only one way to win: **51 f6!**.

It was enough to convince Black to resign in view of 51...gxf6+ 52 ♔f5!.

For example, 52...♔g7 53 ♔e6! wins the f6-pawn and the game.

Or 52...♔e7 53 ♔g6 ♔e6 54 ♔xh6.

Intuition, general principles and memory can take a back seat as a game reaches the final stages.

To put it another way: *Memory* means more in the opening than in other phases of a game. *Intuition* is a star of the middlegame. And the prime time for *calculation* is the endgame.

271. Are there other ways the endgame is very different from earlier phases?

Several. In the late endgame, piece activity declines in significance. A defender may draw a bad-looking position with purely passive moves.

Also, space gradually matters less. A cramped position may turn out to be the best defensive formation. Your opponent can own the rest of the board and not be able to beat you.

Radjabov – Duda

Internet 2021

Black to move

Black is severely cramped and his bishop is bad. Yet he has created an impregnable fortress.

He cannot lose unless he blunders, such as by allowing ♔c5-d6!.

The rest was futile: **55...♔e7 56 ♔c5 ♗f7 57 ♗b5 g6 58 ♔b6 ♗g8 59 ♔c7 ♗f7 60 ♗c6 ♗g8 61 ♗d7 ♗f7 62 ♗c6 ♗g8 63 ♗d7 ♗f7 64 ♗c6 draw**.

For the defender in such equal-material positions, the proper attitude is: "Wait and see." He doesn't need counterplay.

The player with advantage in an endgame, in an early ending or a later one, should also change his attitude.

272. In what way?

Slow down. The endgame mantra is: "Don't hurry."

In the opening, speed carries a lot of weight. The player with the advantage wants to press it before his opponent coordinates his pieces.

But in an endgame, there may be little benefit to rushing events. An extra pawn will remain an extra pawn ten moves from now.

273. How much of a material advantage do I need to win an endgame?

If you have no pawns, you need the equivalent of an extra rook.

This rule has a few exceptions. A king and two bishops may beat a king and knight. A king, rook and bishop will defeat a king and rook if the defender errs. But the exceptions rarely occur.

274. What do I need to win if I still have pawns?

Two extra pawns are usually enough.

One extra pawn will win some endgames but not others. Whether it is enough depends on several factors, such as the total number of pawns on the board.

275. Why?

The more pawns there are, the greater the chances for you to create a winning passed pawn or to win a second extra pawn.

A good illustration of this is an endgame in which each side has a king and one knight:

White to move

With only one pawn on the board Black should have an easy time drawing. He can sacrifice his knight for the pawn. White cannot mate with K+N-versus-K.

If there are two pawns against one, Black's task is somewhat harder. Suppose we add a White pawn at f2 and a Black pawn at f7 to the diagram. Black should still draw if he finds good moves.

But if it is three pawns against two, the outcome depends on whether the superior side has a good passed pawn.

144

White to move

White should win. If Black uses his pieces to stop the b-pawn, White will be freed to try to win a kingside pawn.

However, if the White b2-pawn is on h2 instead, White will have only one winning plan – to create a passed kingside pawn. The game will likely be drawn.

And if it is four pawns against three pawns, it is almost always a win, even if there is no passed pawn yet.

That would be the case if we have White pawns at e3, f2, g2 and h2 and Black pawn at f7, g7 and h7 in the diagram.

You can find some of these positions in endgame textbooks.

276. That leads me to my next question. How much book knowledge do I need?

Some authors claim you must master 100 or more "book" positions to play endgames well. This is not true.

All you really need to know are some of the positions with relatively little material, such as with fewer than six pieces and pawns.

Don't worry about the more complex endgames. Until you are a better than average player, most of your endgames will be pretty one-sided. Either you or your opponent will probably be a minor piece or several pawns ahead.

277. Are there any basic endgames I can learn quickly?

Yes, very quickly. You can master K+P-versus-K in an hour or two.

If a win is possible, you should be able to win it – even if you are playing a computer.

If a draw is possible and you are the defender, you should be able to draw.

278. *What do you mean by if a win is possible?*

When there are only a few pieces and pawns on the board, it is either a forced win or a draw. There are no "White is better" positions.

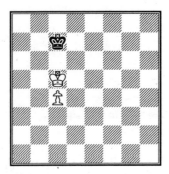

White to move

Black can draw after, for example, **1 ♔d5**, with **1...♚d7**.

The key position arises after **2 c5 ♚c7 3 c6 ♚c8!**.

White can achieve no more than the moral victory of stalemate, **4 ♔d6 ♚d8 5 c7+ ♚c8 6 ♚c6**, as we saw in Question 107.

But if it is Black to move in the diagram, it is a forced loss. This is a vital, must-know difference.

It becomes apparent after **1...♚d7** and **2 ♔b6!**.

The rest could be **2...♚c8 3 c5 ♚b8 4 c6 ♚c8 5 c7 ♚d7 6 ♚b7** and queens.

No different is 1...♚b7 2 ♔d6! or 1...♚c8 2 ♚c6.

279. *Are all king-and-pawn endgames relatively easy?*

No. But there are fewer special techniques and concepts you need to know.

"The square"

This is one of them. If it is White's turn, he queens after 1 a4.

Black is one move late, (1...♔f3 2 a5 ♔e4 3 a6 ♔d5 4 a7 ♔c6 5 a8(♕)+.)

But if it is Black's turn in the diagram, then 1...♔f3! puts his king inside a square bounded by a3-f3-f8-a8.

He would catch the pawn after 2 a4 ♔e4 3 a5 ♔d5 4 a6 ♔c6 5 a7 ♔b7.

Pawn endgames are often decided by pawn races – whoever queens first usually wins.

280. Which endgames with only a few pieces are hardest to learn?

High on the list are those with just queens or with bishops of opposite color. They require subtle understanding and techniques that aren't applicable in other endings.

Rook endings are another story. They have their own difficult concepts and a few "book" positions to know.

As you become more experienced you should study rook endgames more because they occur so often. With or without an extra piece, an endgame of K+R-versus-K+R may happen in nearly half of all endgames.

281. What's the story with basic checkmates?

There are four basic mates you will find in a beginners' book. They fall into extremes.

Two are very easy and common. The other two are very hard and rare.

The easy ones are K+Q-versus-K and K+R-versus-K. They often occur in the games of young players because kids tend to play out lost positions until checkmate.

King and two pieces against a king is very rare at all levels, even in grandmaster games. Nevertheless, those two endings are worth studying.

282. Why?

Because they teach a valuable technique that can be applied to other endgames: How to restrict.

We talked about this in Question 26. Here's how it works in a textbook ending.

White to move

Even GMs continue to play with just a king against a king, bishop and knight. They know they are lost. But the win is so difficult that an opponent may fail to deliver mate in 50 moves and allow them to claim a draw. (For the rule, see Question 321.)

The position in the diagram is an easy version of this ending. Easy, that is, if you understand the technique of restriction: **1 ♘d5!** and **2 ♗b5!**.

This puts the king in a cage of six squares. Winning is now a simple process of using the White king to nudge its rival into the corner.

For example, **1...♚a7 2 ♗b5! ♚b7 3 ♔f2 ♚c8 4 ♔e3 ♚b8 5 ♔d4 ♚b7 6 ♔c5 ♚c8 7 ♔c6 ♚d8 8 ♔d6 ♚c8**.

White to move

You don't need book knowledge of specific moves here. What you need to know is that the Black king should be driven into the corner. The rest is:

9 ♔e7 ♚b7 10 ♔d7 ♚b8 11 ♗a6 ♚a7 12 ♗c8 ♚b8 13 ♘b4 ♚a7 14 ♔c7 ♚a8 15 ♗b7+ ♚a7 16 ♘c6 mate.

283. *What are the other important endgame techniques?*

There are more than a dozen. Among the ones you need to know are winning the opposition, shouldering, blockading, cutting off, creating a mismatch and achieving a breakthrough.

The opposition and shouldering are based on the simplest of rules. The two kings cannot be on adjacent squares.

We saw how Black drew in Question 278 by gaining the opposition and how White won by seizing it. Yet this simple technique can lead to embarrassing errors.

Firouzja – Carlsen

Stavanger 2020

White to move

White played a natural move, **69 ♔c3??**.

But after **69...♔c5!** he resigned because Black had won the opposition.

White's king must give way, e.g. 70 ♔b3 ♔d4 or 70 ♔d3 ♔b4 71 ♔e3 ♔c4.

Of course, White knew all about the opposition. He saw 69 ♔c4?? would lose to 69...♔e6 70 ♔d3 ♔f7 71 ♔e3 ♔g6 72 ♔f3 ♔h5! 73 ♔g3 ♔g5 74 ♔f3 ♔h4!.

But in the diagram he failed to find the drawing 69 ♔d2!. Then 69...♔c5 70 ♔c3! – and it is Black's king that must back off.

Black can set a trap with 69...♔c6 so that 70 ♔c3?? ♔c5 transposes into the game. But 70 ♔c2! draws.

284. *What about blockading?*

Blockading is easier to understand. We know that most endgames are won by queening a pawn. And we know protected pawns tend to grow in value as they get closer to the eighth rank (Question 222).

Therefore, you want to stop your opponent's most advanced pawn by planting a piece in its way.

The blockading piece can usually maintain its place until it is attacked by an inferior piece. Knights are splendid blockaders.

285. Why?

Two reasons. First, a more valuable piece, a queen or a rook, has to give way when threatened by a minor piece. But if a defended knight is attacked by a minor piece, it may be able to remain in place.

Second, if a blockader has to move and allow the pawn to advance, it might have to sacrifice itself for the pawn to stop it from promoting.

This is fatal in a queen or rook ending. But if it is K+N+P-versus-K+N, the knight can give itself up. The result is K+N-versus-K, a draw because of insufficient mating material, as noted in the first diagram in Question 275.

As for the other pieces, a king is a very good blockader and so is a bishop in a bishops-of-opposite-color ending.

The rook is not good at blockading but it is splendid at cutting off.

286. What is cutting off?

This technique literally cuts off the enemy king from taking part in play.

Polugaevsky – Korchnoi

Evian-les-Bains 1977

Black to move

Two moves earlier White could have forced a somewhat easy draw. But after **45...♖e3!** he could resign.

Black's rook can maintain a barrier on the e-file that shuts out White's king. The rest of the game is a losing battle of White's rook against Black's king and pawn.

This illustrates another basic technique, the mismatch.

287. And that is?

It is a mini-endgame within the endgame:

By taking White's king out of play, Black created a final battle of two against one: **46 ♔f4 ♖e1 47 ♖d8 ♔c5 48 ♖c8+ ♔d4.**

One White piece, his rook, had no chances against two Black units, his king and pawn, **49 ♔f3 d5 50 ♔f2 ♖e5 51 ♖a8 ♔c3 52 ♖a3+ ♔b4.**

The rest was **53 ♖a1 d4 54 ♖c1 d3 55 ♖c8 d2 56 ♖b8+ ♔c3 57 ♖c8+ ♔d3 58 ♖d8+ ♔c2 59 ♖c8+ ♔d1.**

White resigned because the position is one of those that all masters know and would-be masters must learn.

288. Why?

Because you might not find the winning method by using common sense or intuition. It's a case when book knowledge rules.

White to move

White was powerless to avoid this kind of position.

Black's king blocks his own pawn. But after any neutral move, such as 60 ♖c7, he can play 60...♖f5+!.

Then 61 ♔e3 ♔e1! allows him to queen.

The key line is 61 ♔g2 ♔e2. White can deliver checks but they run out after 62 ♖e7+ ♔d3 63 ♖d7+ ♔e3 64 ♖e7+ ♔d4 65 ♖d7+ ♖d5!.

The diagram shows what is known as the Lucena position. It is one of the fairly few must-know endgame positions. It is the natural result of many rook endgames in which one player has a single extra pawn.

289. You also mentioned shouldering. What is that?

It is another way of exploiting the rule that says the kings cannot be adjacent to one another.

One king occupies a square and prevents the other king from approaching his goal. It's also been called elbowing and the "hockey technique."

White to move and draw

White is much too late after 1 ♔d5 f5!.

A natural try is 1 ♔f6 because it wins a pawn. Black would lose after 1...♚g4 2 ♔xf7 ♚f4?? 3 ♔e6!.

But Black's king can shoulder White's out with 2...♚f5!. He then wins with ...♚e5-d5-c5xb5.

White should play **1 ♔f5!** instead.

Then 1...♚h6?? 2 ♔f6 wins for him. But **1...♚h4!** 2 ♔f6? ♚g4 3 ♔xf7 ♚f5 again wins for Black.

Therefore, the correct result is a draw after 1 ♔f5! ♚h4!. **2 ♔f4!**.

Black to move

There is no progress in 2...♚h3 3 ♔f3!.

Black even loses after 2...f6?? because he gets shouldered out, 3 ♔f5 ♚g3 4 ♔xf6 ♚f4 5 ♚e6 and ♚d6-c6xb6.

290. What is a breakthrough?

It is the creation of a passed pawn, often in a dramatic manner. It may require the sacrifice of a pawn to make way for another pawn.

M. Muzychuk – Ju Wenjun

Ningbo 2009

Black to move

Black tried to win with a logical move, **51...g5**.

Then 52 hxg5 fxg5 and ...h4 would give her a passed pawn.

White can stop that pawn but would lose on the queenside (53 ♔f3 ♔d4! and ...♔c3).

But 51...g5?? was a blunder because **52 g4!** is a breakthrough. It created a passed h-pawn.

White won after **52...hxg4 53 h5 f5 54 h6**.

Black to move

She can create a second passed pawn 54...♔f6 55 b4! (and eventually c4-c5).

Breakthrough is an important technique in pawn endings. It occurs infrequently when there are other pieces. But some more sophisticated techniques, such as imposing zugzwang, are common in those endings.

291. What is zugzwang?

There is more confusion about this concept than anything else in endgame lore.

Bobby Fischer defined zugzwang as "a forced bad move." But it is really a position, not a move. Zugzwang comes about because you cannot give up your turn to move.

J. Polgar – Kasparov

Dos Hermanas 1996

Black to move

This is an exception to the rule that you need an extra rook to win an endgame without pawns.

It appears to be a draw because White's rook can check.

Black can use his knight to shield his king and would win after 89...♘e6 90 ♖h1+?? ♔g6 91 ♖g1+ ♘g5.

But White is safe after 90 ♔g8!.

There is, however, a win thanks to zugzwang, **89...♖b8+ 90 ♖g8 ♘e8!**.

White to move

There is no Black threat. But any White move loses. For example, 91 ♖g1 ♘f6+.

White resigned in view of 91 ♖f8 ♔g6 92 ♖g8+ ♔f7 93 ♔h7 ♘f6+!.

Technically, this is not a true zugzwang because only one of the players is at a disadvantage by having to move. Black would still be winning if it was his turn, because he could "pass" with 91...♖a8.

292. This seems much too sophisticated for me. Will I ever get to use zugzwang?

You already have. Whenever you win an endgame of K+R-versus-K you probably use the techniques of restricting and zugzwang.

You will also need zugzwang to win most endgames in which you have an extra piece and cannot easily create a passed pawn.

293. Can I use endgame techniques in the middlegame?

Not shouldering or cutoff. But breakthrough and zugzwang can occur.

Podgaets – Dvoretsky

Odessa 1974

Black to move

One way of imposing zugzwang is 29...♖h8! (30 ♖e1 ♘xf2!).

Black preferred **29...♖f3!** so that 30 ♕xf3 ♕h2 mate or 30 ♖e1 ♖xf2.

White resigned after **30 c4 ♔h6!**. Black could continue king moves until White moved a piece and lost.

294. You also mentioned a fortress. Is it possible with queens on the board?

Yes, but it happens more often when one player wins the other guy's queen.

Javakhishvili – Girya

Warsaw 2013

Black to move

There is no more than perpetual check after 57...♘g4+ 58 ♔h3!.

Black played **57...♘f3+** and play went **58 ♕xf3! ♕xf3 59 ♗e1**.

Once White posted his bishop on g5 after ♗d2, Black conceded the draw. No progress is possible.

295. Let's go back to pawns. Does it matter which files they occupy in an endgame?

In some cases. The ones that matter most are rook pawns.

If the only pawn on the board is an a- or h-pawn, you will find it difficult to win a K+R-versus-K+R ending and very difficult to win a K+Q-versus-K+Q ending.

But rook pawns are best when trying to win knight endings.

296. Why knight endings?

A knight has a particularly difficult time stopping a passed rook pawn.

White wins

Black has no defense against ♔b7.

It is very different if we move the position one file over.

If the White pawn is on b7 and his king on d6, then a Black knight on b8 can draw by meeting ♔c7 with …♘a6+!.

It is also worth knowing that connected passed pawns are a big asset in most endings – but not queen endings. Exceptions like that make experience matter a lot in the endgame.

297. I've seen the terms "drawish endgame" and "dead draw." What is the difference?

These are evaluations that masters toss around casually and often carelessly. A more useful term is "drawable."

It means with best play the inferior side can draw.

Short – Korchnoi

Horgen 1995

White to move

A master might shrug as he dismisses this position as "a dead draw."

Another master might hedge by calling it "drawish." He is not predicting what the result would be if the players made the best moves.

In fact, it would be a draw after, for example, 55 ♖g8+.

Then 55…♔h5 56 ♗e2+! f3 allows liquidation to a position that is truly dead.

After 57 ♗xf3+! ♗xf3 58 ♖h8+! and ♖xh4 White can claim a draw due to insufficient material.

298. What is a "book win"?

A position with a winning method you can find in books.

The last example illustrates this. Black had a book win after White blundered with **55 ♖xh4?? ♔xh4.**

White to move

White cannot blockade the pawn for long and can only hope to give up his bishop for it.

Black can win by denying the bishop access to f3. He does it with **56 ♔d2 ♔g3 57 ♗e2 ♗f3! 58 ♗c4 ♗g4! 59 ♗d5 ♗h3 60 ♗e4 ♗g2!**.

Then **61 ♗d3 f3 62 ♔e3 f2 63 ♗c4 ♗d5 64 ♗f1 ♗c6** created zugzwang.

White to move

White resigned because the Black king gets to g1, e.g. **65 ♗c4 ♔g2 66 ♗d3 ♔g1**.

Then another basic technique, deflection, completes the job: **67 ♗c4 ♗g2 68 ♗d3 ♗f1! 69 ♗f5 ♗a6 70 ♗h3 ♗c8!** and queens.

299. Are there simple endgame tips I should remember?

Too many to name all of them. Here are a few:

Rooks should try to occupy the seventh rank.

In queen endgames, a passed pawn is more important than an extra pawn.

Take the opposition in a king and pawn ending.

A knight endgame is a pawn endgame. (The same techniques and principles apply to both.)

Place your rook behind a passed pawn.

300. What's the reasoning behind the last one?

If you place your rook behind your passed pawn, it does three very good things.

The rook (a) protects the pawn, (b) supports its advance and (c) can move along its file without losing its power to protect and support.

This is known as Siegbert Tarrasch's rule.

301. What if my rook is behind my opponent's passed pawn?

That is nearly as good, as this example shows.

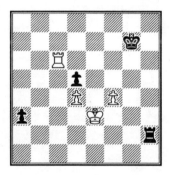

Topalov – Aronian

Monaco 2011

White to move

Following Tarrasch's rule, 43 ♖a6! is the simplest way to draw.

For example, 43...a2 44 ♔d3 and later ♔c3-b3.

Instead, White chose **43 f5**. Black offered a trade of rooks, **43... ♖h6!**.

White could have saved himself by making his rook the more active one, with 44 ♖c7+! ♔f6 45 ♖c5 or 45 ♖d7.

But he chose **44 ♖c1?**. This allowed Black to apply Tarrasch's rule with **44...♖a6!**.

Black threatened to queen in two moves. This prompted **45 ♔d3 a2 46 ♖a1 ♔f6**.

White to move

This is another example of a mismatch. Black is playing with a king and rook and White can only use his king.

For example, 47 ♔e3 ♔xf5 48 ♔f3 wins the opposition. But it is White's king that has to back off after 48...♜a3+ and ...♔e4xd4.

White eventually lost after **47 ♔c3 ♔xf5 48 ♔b2 ♔e4 49 ♜e1+ ♔xd4**.

302. Are there any other common sense rules I should know?

There is one that also makes sense earlier in a game: If you have one bishop, put your pawns on the squares of the opposite color.

Ehlvest – Christiansen

New York 2003

White to move

Black would like to follow the rule with 24...a4!.

But **25 a4!** set up the a5-pawn as a target.

Black could have defended better, such as with 25...♝b2 and ...♝a3-b4.

He lost soon after **25... h5 26 ♜d5! ♝f8 27 ♝b6! ♝h6 28 ♜c7 ♜xc7 29 ♝xc7 ♜c8 30 ♝xa5**.

This rule applies best to endgames with bishops of the same color. If there are bishops of opposite colors, the defender wants his pawns to be protected on the same color squares as his bishop.

But as I said, bishops of opposite color endgames are a different animal.

303. Are there any tactics that are more common in the endgame?

One that stands out is the cross-check. This happens when one player meets a check by interposing a piece that gives check.

This occurs most often in queen endgames. The only way to win some K+Q+P-versus-K+Q endgames is with a cross-check.

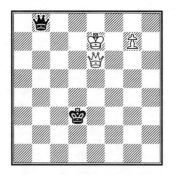

Howell – Ghasi

Hastings 2021

Black to play

Black had prolonged the game by checking the king. But now the queen checks at a7, b7 or c7 would be met by the cross-check 78 ♕d7+!.

After the forced trade of queens that follows, White promotes the pawn.

Instead, Black played **77...♕b4+** and resigned after **78 ♕d6+!**.

Cross-checks may also be important in other endings with queens, such as heavy-piece endings.

304. What is a heavy-piece endgame?

It is one in which the only material left is pawns, queens and rooks.

Matulović – Hübner

Palma de Mallorca 1970

Black to move

Black cannot make clear progress with, for example, 44...♕g3 2 ♖g1.

If he tries to trade queens, 44...♕g5, the rook endgame, 45 ♕xg5 hxg5, is probably won.

But a queen endgame is more certain. Therefore, **44...♖c1!**.

This game lasted another 11 moves: **45 ♕d3+ g6 46 ♕f1 ♖xd1 47 ♕xd1 ♕c4 48 ♕d6 ♕c3 49 f4 b3 50 ♕a3 ♕c2 51 ♕a4 ♕c1+ 52 ♔h2 b2 53 ♕b3 ♕xf4+ 54 ♔g1 ♕c1+ 55 ♔h2 ♔g7.**

White to move

White resigned because he has no checks to stop ...b1(♕).

305. I'm confused about which pieces make winning more likely. Is it knights or rooks or what?

Let's consider the basic case of when there is only one pawn on the board. Then:

The winning chances are best with heavy pieces, just queens or just rooks.

Winning chances are less with just minor pieces because the defender may be able to sacrifice his piece to stop you from queening. The most winnable minor piece endings are K+N+P-versus-K+N and K+B+P-versus-K+N.

Then comes endgames with bishops of the same color. After that, K+N+P-versus-K+B.

The last is K+B+P-versus-K+B of opposite color. There are very few winning chances.

306. Which pieces are best when the pawns are on one wing?

The greatest winning chances are in pure pawn endings – that is, with no pieces besides kings.

The next most-likely win is if there is one knight for each side. The total number of pawns matters, as we saw in Question 275.

In order of declining winnability, the next endgames are K+N-versus-K+B and K+Q-versus-K+Q (a 50-50 chance of winning).

It is less than 50 percent for K+R-versus-K+R.

Then comes K+B-versus-K+N and K+B-versus-K+B of the same color.

There are virtually no chances with bishops of opposite color, barring a blunder.

307. So, in some cases a knight has a better chance of beating a bishop than a bishop has of beating a knight?

Yes, if all the pawns are on one wing. The short-range piece can reach more important squares than the long-range piece.

The short-range knight can reach more important squares than the long-range bishop

White has somewhat better chances of winning in a case like this than if he had a bishop on f3 and Black had a knight at f6.

But with an outside passed pawn for White, the picture changes dramatically.

He would win if we move the e3-pawn to b3 and have the same piece placement (White bishop on f3 and Black knight on f6).

Endgames are that subtle. That's why experience counts most in the endgame.

308. You said rook endgames have the most text book theory. What are the positions I need to know most of all?

There are two, and they are known as the Lucena and Philidor positions.

We already saw the Lucena in Question 288. Here is the Philidor.

White to move

This kind of position has been known since André Philidor analyzed it more than 200 years ago.

One way to draw is 1 ♖h3, to create a cutoff on the third rank.

The rook stays on the rank until Black plays …f3.

Then the rook goes to a distant square on its file. For example, 1…f3 2 ♖h8.

White can give check after check along the files. Black's king has no convenient place to go because he gave up f3 as a haven when he pushed the pawn.

309. My opponent said I couldn't dance at two weddings. I can't dance at all. What did he mean?

He was alluding to an old expression. It means a defender loses when he cannot stop two winning plans at the same time.

Vachier-Lagrave – Dominguez

Internet 2021

Black to move

White has two ways of winning:

One is to push his passed pawn after 43 ♗a6 and 44 b7.

The other is to invade the kingside with his king. Black couldn't stop both.

He eliminated the dangerous pawn with **42...♚c6 43 ♔e5! ♚xb6.**

But he couldn't stop the other winning plan after **44 ♔d6!** and ♔e7.

310. *Is there an easy way to study the endgame?*

Sorry. The easy lessons end when you master K+P-versus-K.

The least painful way to go further is to learn the techniques we mentioned.

Don't worry about the difference between the Lucena position and the Philidor position until you are much better.

The great English chess columnist Leonard Barden wrote a book about endgames. In it, he said he never had to play the Lucena position until he encountered it in the British Championship.

311. *OK, is there at least an easy way to practice playing endgames?*

Yes, thanks to computers you can train yourself in almost all of the major kinds of endings.

A good way to start is with a rook ending. Set up a position like this on your computer and try to beat the machine with the White pieces.

White to move

This is helpful because you need to know, in general, how to win endgames with two extra pawns.

If this is too hard, try adding another White pawn at f2.

If this becomes too easy, add another White pawn but also add a Black one, say at b5.

But remember: Don't hurry.

Chapter Fourteen: How Games End

312. How do draws most often come about?

There are five ways to draw. The most common, by far, is by agreement of the two players. The rarest is stalemate.

313. How rare is that?

Stalemate occurs about 1 percent of the time in tournament games, according to databases.

This typically occurs well into an endgame. There are composed games that end in fewer than a dozen moves. In real games, the shortest known to end in stalemate is:

Sibilio – Mariotti

Ravenna 1982

1 e4 e6 2 ♘f3 d5 3 e5 c5 4 b4 cxb4 5 d4 ♘h6 6 a3 bxa3 7 c3 ♘f5 8 ♘xa3 ♘c6 9 ♘b5 a6! 10 g4 ♗d7 11 ♗g5 ♗e7 12 gxf5 axb5 13 fxe6 fxe6 14 ♖xa8 ♕xa8 15 ♖g1 ♕a3 16 ♗xb5 ♗xg5 17 ♖xg5 ♕xc3+ 18 ♔f1 0-0 19 ♗xc6 ♗xc6 20 ♔g2 ♗a4! 21 ♕e2 ♗c2! 22 ♘e1 ♗e4+ 23 f3 ♖xf3? 24 ♘xf3 ♗xf3+ 25 ♕xf3 ♕d2+ 26 ♔h3 ♕xg5

White to move

Black could have won slowly, such as with 23...♗g6. But he chose a combination to reach this apparently winning endgame.

However, he allowed **27 ♕f8+! ♔xf8** draw.

More common ways of drawing are by perpetual check (about 10 per cent of database games) and by other versions of repetition of position (5 per cent).

314. Do many tournament games end in checkmate?

Database figures vary but the range is 2 to 4 percent of games.

Fewer than 2 per cent of decisive games were lost due to forfeitures, either on time or by failure to show up for the game.

315. How should I offer a draw?

"Draw?" or "I offer a draw" are common methods.

In a tournament game, you should offer a draw as you make a move, not when you or your opponent is thinking.

It is discourteous to offer a draw in a lost position. It is also ill-mannered to offer a draw repeatedly after your opponent declines your first offer.

316. What is the proper way to decline?

A simple "No" is sufficient.

"I would like to play on" is more courteous.

If you silently make a move instead, this means you decline. But many of your opponents will consider this rude behavior.

317. Are there devious draw offers?

Yes. For example, a player can say, "Are you playing for a win?"

If his opponent replies "Yes," the first player can say he wasn't offering a draw. In this way he can detect a lack of ambition in his opponent.

318. Should I offer a draw if I think the position is equal?

You won't learn anything that way. When you are starting out in chess, it is better to play on until there are no real winning chances.

And no real winning chances means a lack of material or a hopelessly locked position. Even if there are few winning chances, offering a draw is an excuse to skip school.

319. How did offering a draw begin?

No one knows. "Dead-drawn" positions were known in an earlier incarnation of chess, but the evidence of draw offers then is lacking.

Bowdler – Philidor

London 1783

White to move

This is one of the oldest recorded draws. Neither side can make progress and a draw was agreed.

In recent years, some tournament organizers have imposed severe restrictions to reduce the number of quick draws.

Under one set of rules, the only permissible draws are by stalemate, repetition of the position and insufficient mating material.

A less stringent set of rules allows draw offers but not before 30 moves have been made.

320. Why do so many grandmaster games end in draws?

The generous answer is that grandmasters defend too well to be defeated.

This may explain why they draw games that last 50 moves. But it does not explain draws in fewer than 30 moves, the much-derided "grandmaster draws."

Those are more a matter of fear and laziness. There have even been games that ended in fewer than five moves.

321. When can I claim a draw according to the rules?

When your opponent has insufficient material to mate you, when the position has been repeated three times or when 50 moves have gone by without a capture or a pawn advance.

Tournament rules are often confusing. Save your questions for Chapter Seventeen.

Chapter Fifteen: Defending

322. I don't like defending. How can I avoid it?

You can't. Some positions demand it. Either you defend or you lose.

You are no different from most people who play this game: We attack because we like to. We defend because we have to, as Fred Reinfeld put it.

323. Isn't good defense just common sense and general principles?

That is somewhat true of attacking but not defending.

Good defense is often illogical and requires strange-looking moves.

Svidler – Kramnik

Khanty-Mansyisk 2014

Black to move

The logical move is 45...♕xe5.

But it would lose to a combination, 46 ♕xe5 fxe5 47 ♖xf8+! ♔xf8 49 ♗c5.

Then 49...♔e7 50 ♗xb4 and 51 ♗xd6 leads to a winning king-and-pawn endgame.

Yet Black saved himself with the counter-intuitive **45...f5!!**.

The tactical point is 46 ♖xf5? ♕xg4+ drops a rook.

Much harder to see is **46 gxf5 ♖f6!**.

White to move

Black has prepared 47...♕e4 with its threat of 48...g4 and 48...♖xf5.

White could not play 47 exf6?? ♕xe8, so a draw occurred after **47 ♔g3 ♕e4 48 ♗c5 ♕e1+ 49 ♗f2 ♕e4!**.

324. I know the queen is my best piece for attacking. Which pieces are best for defending?

The best defenders are the weakest pieces.

This follows a fundamental tenet called the principle of economy. The defender should make the least concession necessary to meet an attack. This takes the form of several don'ts, such as:

(a) Don't commit a major piece to defense when a lesser one will do.

(b) Don't give up material if you can defend otherwise.

(c) Don't make unnecessary pawn moves, such as around your king.

325. There must be a lot of exceptions to these rules, right?

There are *always* exceptions to chess rules.

In regard to (a), a queen move is best if it both defends and counterattacks.

As for (b), you can give up material if you get good counterplay as a result.

And in terms of (c), a well-timed pawn move can make a king safe and free your pieces from defending it.

326. What can I do when I see my opponent preparing to attack my king?

There are three basic responses:

Your king can flee. You can counterattack elsewhere. Or you can contest the danger zone.

Navara – Kramnik

Prague 2008

Black to move

Given time for g3-g4, White would have a powerful attack.

But Black fled the area with **34...♔f7! 35 g4 ♔e8!**.

There was nothing for White to attack in the abandoned wing after **36 ♖h2 ♔d7 37 ♘g3 ♕f7 38 ♔g2 fxg4 39 ♗e3 ♖h8 40 ♖xh8 ♖xh8**.

The second policy is to counterattack on another sector of the board. If the attacker is taking aim at your kingside, shoot at his queenside.

Or try to seize the center. Normally, an attack succeeds only if the center is closed or in the hands of the attacker.

327. What about the third response to a wing attack?

An opponent attacks on a wing when there are favorable factors there. He may have more pieces in the area or the pawn structure gives him more space.

But you can try to change this by bringing in reinforcement pieces or by dissolving the unfavorable part of the pawn structure.

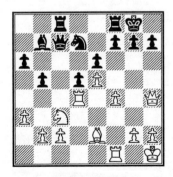

Karjakin – Carlsen

Wijk aan Zee 2010

Black to move

White is prepared to attack the kingside with 19 ♖f3 and 20 ♖h3.

Black cannot defend against ♕xh7 mate with ...♘f6 because it would be captured by the e5-pawn.

But **18...f6!** deprived White of the crucial e5-pawn.

After **19 ♗d3 h6 20 exf6 ♖xf6**, White's f4-pawn was much weaker than Black's king.

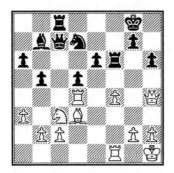

White to move

Black took over the attack and won following **21 f5 ♖cf8 22 ♖g1 ♘c5 23 fxe6 ♘xe6 24 ♖g4 ♘f4 25 ♕g3 ♕e7 26 ♖xf4 ♖xf4**.

328. What are the best techniques of defense?

In many cases they are the reverse of the best techniques of attack.

The attacker tries to open files and diagonals he can use to mount threats. The defender wants to close them and prevent other potentially dangerous lines from being opened.

Smyslov – Botvinnik

World Championship match,
Moscow 1958

Black to move

White has a dangerous attack brewing from ♖h4 and hxg6 or ♖xg4.

Computers say Black should prepare a counterattack with 18...♕d6, followed by 19...♖b8 and ...♕b4.

A good alternative is **18...g5**, so that the h-file cannot be opened by hxg6.

Black was quite safe after **19 ♗xg5 ♕d6 20 ♖h4 ♘f6 21 ♗xf6 ♕xf6 22 ♖xg4+ ♔h8**.

Trading pieces is another example of reversing the attacker's techniques. The defender should try to trade off the most dangerous enemy pieces. An exchange of queens will kill most attacks.

Also, the defender should blockade enemy passed pawns before they become dangerous. The defender should repair a weakness before it becomes fatal.

There are also times when it pays to let an opponent's attacking pawn stay on the board because it serves as a wall of defense.

329. How does that happen?

This exploits a rule that is so obvious no one mentions it. You cannot capture your own pawns. Here is how the defender can use this.

Aronian – Ding Liren

Internet 2021

Black to move

White's attack looks ferocious. He would win after 17...♞xh7?? because the h-file is fully opened for 18 ♕h2!.

But **17...♚h8!** kept the file closed, thanks to White's pawn.

Black can take that pawn when it is safer. If he keeps two extra pawns he should win without much difficulty.

The game later became double-edged, and a critical position arose when the winning chances were equal. Black made the mistake of capturing the pawn that had protected him.

Black to move

White was desperate to open lines. For example, 25...dxe5? 26 ♖d8! and wins.

Black played **25...♔xh7??** and was lost after **26 ♕d3+!** and **27 exd6**.

330. Seems like a lot of calculating for a defender.

That is the norm. The defender typically needs to calculate *more* than the attacker.

331. Why? Attackers cite all sorts of ten-move variations when they annotate their wins.

Those are often variations that their computer showed them after the game.

An attacker can make many moves based on general principles. The defender cannot afford to rely on generalities. The cost of a mistake is much higher for him.

If the attacker errs, the worst that may happen is his advantage will disappear. But if the defender errs, the cost may be disastrous.

Ghasi – Flear

Hastings 2021

Black to move

White has sacrificed a rook on e6. But he has forked all three Black heavy pieces and also threatens ♗xd5.

He would win after 26...♕e7 27 ♕xc5, for example.

But **26...♘f4!** turns the tables, based on 27 ♘xc7 ♘e2+ and ...♘xd4.

Black won after **27 ♕xc5 ♘xe6!**.

332. When a game is over, do computers usually confirm that an attack should have succeeded?

More often they prove the opposite.

They demonstrate there was a defensive resource that would have either blunted the attack or summoned up enough counterplay to put the outcome in question. For example:

Duda – Grandelius

Wijk aan Zee 2021

White to move

Black has a powerful kingside attack brewing, with ...♖e5-h5.

He won after **24 ♕d1 ♖e5! 25 ♘f4 g5!** and then **26 h3 ♕d7**, in view of 27 ♘h5 ♕xh3 mate.

But computers showed how White missed his opportunity for counterplay, with 24 ♕a5!.

Then if Black continued as in the game, 24...♖e5 25 ♘f4 g5, White can respond 26 ♕c7!.

Black to move

Black is the one getting mated, on g7, after 26...gxf4? 27 gxf4 ♕-moves.

333. I think I understand 24 ♕a5. But what exactly is counterplay?

Masters say they know it when they see it. They can't define it precisely, except to say that it means generating threats.

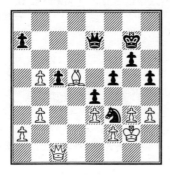

Arkell – Jones

Hastings 2021

Black to move

With so few pieces and fewer White weaknesses, threats by Black seem unlikely.

Black can attack the unprotected bishop (...♕d6, for example) but he really needs something additional.

He found **35...h4!** with prospects of ...hxg3 or ...g5-g4.

That should not have worked. But after **36 ♕c3+? ♔h7 37 a4?** he had made **37...♕d6!** a dangerous move.

White to move

White would be in trouble after 38 ♕c4 hxg3 39 fxg3 ♔h6 and ...♘e5!.

He chose **38 ♗c4??** and would have been lost after **38...♕d1!**, e.g. 39 ♗f1 ♘d2.

334. What if there is no counterplay?

The next best thing is distraction. Grandmaster Yefim Geller described this as "clutching" at your opponent's pieces.

Try to inhibit them, limit them, threaten them when possible.

335. A lot of openings have the word "defense" in their title. Does that mean they are defensive?

Not at all.

Openings named "defense" usually arise when Black does not answer 1 e4 with 1...e5 or 1 d4 with 1...d5.

Two or more centuries ago, the French Defense and Sicilian Defense first gained attention. They were regarded as defensive because they did not allow the usual tactics for White after 1 e4 e5 that began with ♗c4 and possibly ♘f3-g5 and ♕h5.

336. Is there a proper attitude when defending?

Be confident, if not fearless.

It can sow doubts in your opponent's mind. After all, he isn't sure his attack will succeed.

Anand – Beliavsky

Belgrade 1997

Black to move

White's threats include 17 g5!. Black would be lost after 17...♘xh5 18 ♖xh5! gxh5 19 ♘xh5 and ♘f6+, for example.

Instead, he played **17...♘fxg4?!! 17 fxg4 g5.**

It's a crazy idea. But it was bold enough to frighten White into thinking his queen had no escape from h6 and could become trapped.

The game went **18 ♘xe6 fxe6 19 ♖df1 ♖f8 20 ♘d1** and then **20... ♖f7!.**

White to move

Black threatens to win the queen after 21...♖df8, e.g. 22 ♖fg1 ♖f4 and ...♘f7.

White's advantage would be slim after 21 ♘e3 ♖df8 because he has no way of breaking the kingside vice.

Black's fearlessness succeeded when White chose **21 ♗c4** and a draw was agreed soon after **21...♖xf1 22 ♖xf1 ♘xc4**.

Yes, White missed ways to win, such as 18 ♘d3 and ♘xe5.

But Black's boldness was rewarded, as it often is when a player refuses to lose routinely.

337. Seems like a lot to learn. How much time should I devote to studying defense?

A lot – once you are joining the ranks of average players. Before that, learn how to attack better. You can apply what you learn more easily. And attacking is a lot more fun.

Chapter Sixteen: Style

338. I've read about the different playing styles of grandmasters. Do I have a style?

Probably. But you may not be able to tell what it is yet.

Most of your moves will be the same ones that most players will play. But there are telltale moments when you make significant decisions that indicate a style:

Did you grab material or play for mate? Did you go with your gut feeling about a move or choose a move you could calculate more clearly? Did you make a risky sacrifice or play conservatively?

The three Polgar sisters developed their move preferences early. Their father concluded a player's style can be formed by age ten. But it takes a while before your preferences are consistent enough to be called a style.

339. How do I get a style?

The first books and Web sites you read should make a big impression.

World champion Vladimir Kramnik said there were few chess books at his local library when he was growing up. He found a collection of Anatoly Karpov's games and studied it deeply.

"It is quite possible that my style would have been completely different if my first book had been a games collection of [Garry] Kasparov," Kramnik said.

Kramnik – Chjumachenko

Gelendzhik 1987

1 e4 c5 2 f4 b6 3 c4 ♗b7 4 ♘c3 e6 5 ♘f3 d6 6 d4 cxd4 7 ♘xd4 ♘f6 8 ♗d3 ♘bd7 9 ♕e2 ♗e7 10 0-0 0-0 11 ♔h1 ♕c7 12 f5 e5 13 ♘db5 ♕d8 14 ♘d5! ♘xd5 15 exd5! a6 16 ♘c3 ♗f6 17 ♗e3 ♖c8 18 ♘e4 ♘c5 19 ♗xc5! bxc5 20 ♕d2

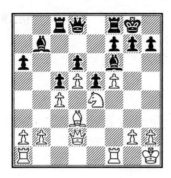

Black to move

By creating a favorable pawn structure, with a knight outpost at e4, Kramnik had eliminated counterplay. This fits in with Karpov's style.

Kramnik had a free hand to prepare a decisive plan of g2-g4-g5.

20... ♖b8 21 a3 a5 22 g4! h6 23 h4! ♗xh4 24 f6 ♗c8 25 ♕h2 ♖b3 26 ♗c2 ♖xb2 27 ♕xh4 ♖xc2 28 g5 ♕d7 29 fxg7 ♕h3+ 30 ♕xh3 ♗xh3 31 gxf8♕ ♔xf8 32 ♖f2 resigns.

340. Would a teacher mold my style?

Certainly. The young Mikhail Tal was trained by one of Latvia's greatest tacticians. Tal became a tactician.

The young Tigran Petrosian had a teacher who revered the classical approach of José Capablanca. Petrosian adopted the classical style.

But personality also plays a role. If Tal and Petrosian had somehow traded teachers, Tal might have become much less daring. But he would likely have his own sense of acceptable risk.

Petrosian might have become much less conservative, but he would still have his innate caution. And neither would likely have become as strong as they eventually did.

341. What did you mean by a classical style?

This is an approach popularized by José Capablanca, Siegbert Tarrasch and Wilhelm Steinitz, among other great players.

They emphasized general principles, avoiding pawn weaknesses and accumulating positional assets that can be exploited in the endgame.

Menchik – Capablanca
Hastings 1930-1

1 d4 ♘f6 2 ♘f3 b6 3 e3 ♗b7 4 ♗d3 c5 5 0-0 ♘c6 6 c3 e6 7 ♘e5 d6 8 ♘xc6 ♗xc6 9 ♕e2 ♗e7 10 ♗b5 ♕d7 11 ♗xc6 ♕xc6 12 ♘d2 0-0

13 dxc5 dxc5 14 e4 ♖ad8 15 e5 ♘d5 16 ♘f3 ♖d7! 17 ♖d1 ♖fd8 18 ♗d2
b5! 19 ♔f1 ♘b6 20 ♗f4 h6 21 ♖xd7 ♖xd7 22 ♖d1 ♖xd1+ 23 ♕xd1 ♕e4!

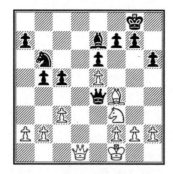

White to move

Black has followed classical principles – doubling rooks on the only open file, seizing space on the queenside and centralizing his queen.

This paid off. He will win a pawn because of the threats of …♕xf4 and …♕c4+/…♕xa2.

None of these steps is difficult to understand. This is why this style is popular with students.

When a classical-style player, such as Vishy Anand or Bobby Fischer, won like this, chess can seem like a simple game.

24 ♗g3 ♕c4+ 25 ♕e2 ♕xe2+ 26 ♔xe2 ♘a4 27 ♔d2 ♘xb2 28 ♔c2 ♘c4 29 ♘d2 ♘xd2 30 ♔xd2 c4! 31 ♗f4 a6 32 ♗e3 ♔f8 33 ♗b6 ♔e8 34 ♔e3 ♔d7 35 ♔d4 ♔c6 36 ♗a7 f5 37 a4 g6 38 f4 h5 39 axb5+ ♔xb5 40 g3 a5 41 ♔e3 ♗c5+ 42 ♗xc5 ♔xc5 43 White resigns

The classical style replaced the more carefree Romantic style.

342. What was romantic about it?

Not much. The name came about because it was the popular style during the heyday of the Romantic schools of music and art in the early 19th century.

Romantic players, such as Adolf Anderssen, valued the attack. Sacrifices were king. The "Immortal Game" and the "Evergreen Game," both wins by Anderssen, were regarded as the height of chess achievement. When you make a "real" sacrifice, you might feel like a Romantic.

MacDonnell – Bird

London 1874

1 e4 e5 2 f4 exf4 3 ♘f3 g5 4 h4 g4 5 ♘e5 h5 6 ♗c4 ♘h6 7 d4 d6
8 ♘d3 f3 9 g3 f5 10 ♘c3 fxe4 11 ♘xe4 ♘f5 12 ♔f2 ♗e7 13 ♘f4 ♖h7

14 ♘g6 d5! 15 ♘xe7 dxe4 16 ♘d5? ♗e6! 17 ♗g5!

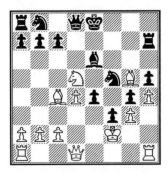

Black to move

17...♗xd5! 18 ♗xd8? e3+ 19 ♔g1 ♗xc4 20 ♗g5 f2+ 21 ♔h2 e2 22 ♕d2

Now 22...♘c6 is the easiest way to win. Instead, Black threw away his advantage. But the idea of two straight under-promotions charmed his Romantic contemporaries:

22...f1(♘)+? 23 ♖hxf1 exf1(♘)+ 24 ♖xf1 ♗xf1 25 ♕e1+ ♘e7 26 ♕xf1? ♘bc6 27 d5 ♖f7 28 ♕c4 ♘e5 29 ♕xc7 ♘f3+ 30 ♔g2 ♖c8 31 ♕a5 ♖xc2+ 32 ♔f1 ♘xg5+ 33 ♔e1 ♘f3+ 34 ♔d1 ♖d2+ 35 ♔c1 ♘xd5 36 a3 ♖c7+ 37 ♔b1 ♘c3+! 38 bxc3 ♖e7 39 White resigns.

In the Romantic era, the success of an attack was ascribed to the imagination of the attacker, not the failure of the defender. Few noticed that White could have saved the game with 26 ♕e4!, followed by 27 ♕xh7 or 27 ♕xb7.

Romantic beliefs were overthrown by Steinitz, who showed that successful attacks are based on positional advantages, such as a lead in development. But many of Steinitz's views were, in turn, challenged by the Hypermodern school.

343. Why was it called that?

Steinitz's theories were dubbed the "Modern School," so what followed was called "Hypermodern," by Savielly Tartakower.

It seemed radical because Hypermodern players appeared to disregard the center with their opening moves. In fact, the opposite was true:

They valued the center so much that they felt it was a mistake to occupy it quickly with pawns that would become targets. Instead, they investigated openings such as the Réti Opening and the King's Indian, Queen's Indian, Grünfeld and Alekhine's defenses.

These openings remain popular, and Hypermodern ideas have blended into today's dominant style.

344. What is it called?

When grandmasters are asked to describe their style they give answers such as "active" and "dynamic."

Strangely, no one describes themselves as "passive" and "lethargic."

345. But what do they mean by "dynamic"?

It can mean choosing moves that benefit piece play rather than static features such as pawn structure. A dynamic player is focused more on how a position can change in the next few moves than by its enduring qualities.

For example, Garry Kasparov was considered more dynamic than Anatoly Karpov. Karpov "finds the lasting weakness more important than losing the initiative," said Jan Timman, a frequent opponent of the two Ks.

In contrast, for Kasparov, "Concepts such as shattered pawn structures lose their relevance when there is a chance to launch a heavy offensive," Timman said.

Karpov famously said, "I have no style." But he is usually considered a "positional" player.

346. What is that?

This is also hard to define, even by the masters who say it is their style.

Steinitz said positional play was the accumulation of small advantages. Aron Nimzovich vigorously denied this. He said positional play meant preventing the opponent from making good moves.

A third definition says positional play simply means strengthening your position when you can't attack and when you don't need to defend.

347. Is a player's style reflected in all phases of a game?

No. Style is detected when you make a choice of reasonable moves. When the task becomes more technical – such as queening a pawn – that choice is narrowed.

As a result, there is no Hypermodern or Romantic way to play the endgame.

348. Do today's grandmasters have distinctive styles?

The best description of them is "eclectic." They differ from one another but in much more subtle ways.

If you showed an educated player the score of two games, without the names of the players, he could tell the one played by Capablanca from the one played by Morphy. Or a Petrosian game from a Tal game.

But he would probably be stumped if you showed him games played by two of the world's elite grandmasters today and asked him to tell you something about the players.

349. *What other factors go into a style?*

There are distinguishing marks such as how a player feels about material and how willing he is to take risks.

Some players are unabashed materialists. "The best thing about playing chess is taking your opponent's pieces," said Yasser Seirawan. "That's the fun part of the game."

Even Bobby Fischer, who made several celebrated sacrifices, was a materialist at heart.

Najdorf – Fischer

Havana 1966

Black to move

Black has a safe and sound candidate move in 31...♕f6.

Few of Fischer's colleagues would have played the risky **31...♘xd5** because Black's king and queen are lined up in an enduring pin after **32 ♗c4! ♕e6**.

But Fischer was convinced he could relieve the pressure, **33 ♗c3 ♗c6 34 ♕b3 ♔f7 35 ♕b8 ♘g8 36 h3 ♘ge7 37 ♕h8 ♕h6**.

And that freed him to grab another pawn, **38 ♘e2 ♗xa4**. He went on to win.

"Concentrate on material gains" instead of checkmate, Fischer advised young players. "Whatever your opponent gives you, take, unless you see a good reason not to." (See Question 257 for the opposite point of view.)

350. Can I fit into more than one category?

Yes. You can be a dynamic materialist. Or a risk-taking positional player. You might play 1 ♘f3 but with the idea of a quick mating attack.

Tarrasch is often described as a classical player. That sounds like he avoided potentially weak pawns. But he ridiculed that kind of player. "He who fears to have an isolated d-pawn should give up chess," he declared.

There are also different styles based on factors that have less to do with the position on the board than with personality.

351. How so?

One of the basic differences in style is between pragmatists and perfectionists. Or you can call them thinkers and *players*.

Thinkers understand chess better than they play it. They enjoy the intellectual debate of chess, the process of searching for the absolutely best move.

But the process takes time and means they frequently get into time trouble. Lev Polugaevsky was a world-class player but conceded he was "too artistic" to become world champion.

In contrast, *players* enjoy chess as a game, akin to a sport. Anatoly Karpov is one of the best examples of this.

If you "play the man, not the board," you are more player than thinker.

352. What does "play the man" mean?

It means using all you know about the human sitting opposite you:

Is he getting short of time and vulnerable to a trap? Have his previous moves indicated he is more of a positional player than a tactician?

These factors can steer you away from choosing the move you might consider objectively best. Instead, you might pick the move that works best against *this* opponent under *these* circumstances.

In the following position White is in trouble because Black threatens to trap his g3-bishop with 25...f4.

"If I were playing against a computer then it would conduct the position to victory in ten times out of ten," Vladimir Kramnik said after the game. "But I am not playing a computer."

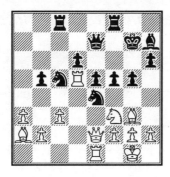

Kramnik – Harikrishna

Shamkir 2017

White to move

He chose **25 ♖xe5?** because it was harder – for a human – to find the best defense.

Initially Black did, **25....dxe5 26 ♗xe5+ ♘f6 27 ♕xb5 ♖fd8**, and he was close to winning.

But he soon made minor errors, **29 h3 ♖b8 30 ♕e2 ♗g8? 31 ♗b1 ♕b7 32 b4 ♖e8 33 c4 ♕c6?**.

Kramnik carefully steered his way to victory, **34 ♕b2 ♖bd8 35 c5 ♕e6 36 b5 ♔f8 37 c6 g4 38 hxg4 fxg4 39 ♗xe4 gxf3 40 ♗xf6 ♖d6 41 ♗g7+ ♔f7 42 ♗e5 resigns**.

If you think chess is a science, you would not play like this. But if you think it is more like a sport, you might.

353. What if you think chess is an art?

That is another style. Yuri Averbakh, the great Russian authority, had his own way of describing different styles and he called one of them the *artists*. They want to win games elegantly.

In contrast, he said, *killers* want to beat their opponents quickly.

Fighters are not that extreme but summon up all their strength to win, Averbakh said. They think about chess all the time. They are unlike *sportsmen,* who forget about chess when a game is over. Their day at the office is done.

Averbakh also identified a style he called the *researchers*. They think of chess as a science. They investigate openings and endgames to find new ideas. Polugaevsky and Mikhail Botvinnik were researchers.

354. I've heard someone called a coffeehouse player. What's that?

That's a derogatory term for someone who often wins with a simple tactical trick, typically in a bad position.

The hustlers you may see in public parks are "coffeehouse players." Few of them are masters.

Masters may seem to be playing in a coffeehouse style when they take a calculated risk.

355. How would you describe a calculated risk?

It means using cost-benefit analysis of a move, not just purely chess analysis.

Bent Larsen, who thrived on this risk-taking, explained it to Tigran Petrosian:

"Take any three games. If I play them the way you do – correctly – I will score one and a half points. But if I play them as I do, then in one of the three I may be punished. But even then I will score two points out of three."

Don't feel that you have to choose a style. For the vast majority of players, it is not a choice but a natural reflection of how they want to play chess. Just try to make the best decisions and your style will eventually reveal itself.

Chapter Seventeen: Rulebook

356. Why does White move first?

No one knows for certain. The best explanation for this rule is that the White pieces were once considered unlucky.

This goes back to when chess was played mainly in clubs. Before a game began, one of the players might hide a black pawn in one hand and a white one in the other and ask his opponent to choose a hand. This seemed fairer than to allow someone to have his choice of color in every game because many players would pick the "luckier" black pieces.

There was also a convention in many clubs that called for a separate drawing to determine who played the first move. As a result, a player could have Black *and* move first. That is what happened in some of Adolf Anderssen's brilliancies in the mid-19th century. It is believed the "Immortal Game" began **1...e5 2 e4 f5 3 exf5 ♝c5 4 ♛h5+ ♚f8**.

White to move

When tournament chess began in the middle of the 19th century, this procedure fell out of favor. A new convention came about: To compensate for being unlucky, White moved first. It seemed like a fair compromise.

357. I received a fancy chess set as a present. Can I use it in tournaments?

Check with tournament officials. In many tournaments, your opponent can object if the set does not resemble the standard "Staunton" design.

So, if you show up to play with a set based on Star Trek characters, Greek gods, Roman emperors or The Simpsons, you will probably be out of luck.

358. Can pieces be too small for the board in a tournament?

Too small or too large. A disproportionate set of pieces would probably be vetoed by your opponent.

The United States Chess Federation (USCF) lists standards that are followed in many countries: The square size should be anywhere from 2 inches to 2.5 inches, while the king's height should be 3.375 inches to 4.5 inches. The standard USCF tournament set has 2.25 inch squares and a king's height of 3.75 inches.

359. Are there rules about the color of the squares?

About a thousand years ago, chess was played on a monochromatic board. So was checkers. (A "checkerboard" wasn't checkered.)

Today, tournament rules refer to the squares as "white" and "black." But the only widely accepted rule is that half of the squares must be lighter in color than the others.

360. Are there board colors that are considered best?

The most common boards used in tournaments are buff or cream-colored and green. You will also find boards with red, burgundy, blue, purple, even pink squares. But your opponent may object to playing on one of them.

Tournament boards are rarely wooden. For convenience, they are often vinyl boards you can roll up and carry easily.

361. Are the pieces usually white and black?

Black, yes. But tournament players prefer off-white or wood-colored pieces. They want a color contrast between the pieces and the board. This makes it easier on their eyes. And they prefer pieces with a dull finish, not a shiny one.

It is believed that in the oldest surviving game using the modern rules, "White" used red pieces and "Black" used green pieces. We don't know what the board looked like in the game (Question 27).

362. Once the game starts can I adjust the pieces on their squares?

Yes, but only when it is your turn to move and after you say "*J'adoube*."

This is a strange convention because it comes from a somewhat obsolete French verb. It is used to mean "I am adjusting."

If you repeatedly adjust pieces when your opponent's clock is running, this is unsportsmanlike and you could be penalized.

363. I played an opponent who said the knights should face forward. True?

Untrue. Knights are the only pieces that usually have a front and back and can "face." There is no right or wrong way to position them as long as they are within their squares.

Garry Kasparov placed his knights facing left. Others say they should face one another. You get to choose how your knights face.

364. Are there players who announce a check?

Almost no one does in today's tournaments.

It used to be considered a courtesy to say "Check" when attacking a king. But there is no rule governing it.

Of course, if your opponent ignores a check, you should point this out and make him take the move back.

It was once considered polite to announce when you threaten to capture your opponent's queen, by saying "*Garde la dame.*" No longer.

365. Is there a limit on the number of checks you can make in a game?

If the *same* checks are given over and over in the *same* position, this is perpetual check. It is a form of "repetition of the position." Either you or your opponent can claim a draw.

But if the checks are not exactly the same ones, a player can keep checking. This is common in endgames in which one or both of the players have a queen and little else.

A game in the Czech Under-16 Girls Championship saw 74 consecutive checks. That may be a record.

366. What about a limit on the number of moves by the same piece?

There is no such rule.

In some endgames the defender has nothing to do but shift a piece back and forth.

For example, in this position, Black played **53...♖e1**, the fifth move by this rook.

I. Nikolić – Arsović

Belgrade 1989

Black to move

He kept moving it. The same position did not occur three times, so he could not claim a draw under "repetition of position." He moved the rook 148 more times before a draw was agreed.

This set a record for most moves by the same piece in a game. It is also the longest recorded game, 259 moves, according to Tim Krabbé, a renowned collector of chess oddities.

367. What is the limit on the length of a game?

There is none, per se. But there is a 50-move rule:

If neither player makes a capture or advances a pawn in the course of 50 moves, a draw can be claimed by either player.

368. Sounds arbitrary. Why 50 moves and not 100?

It was 75 moves under the rules of the earlier version of chess. But in that game the queen was a very weak piece, and delivering mate was much more difficult. Fifty moves seemed a more appropriate way to prevent a player from keeping a game going with just the hope of a blunder.

Skripchenko – Gaponenko

Russian Women's Blitz
Championship 2010

Black to move

Black played **161...♗f2+??**. It was the 50th move without a capture.

Before White could play 162 ♖xf2! an arbiter stepped in and declared a draw.

369. How do you prove 50 moves have been played?

With your scoresheet. If you are not keeping score, because of a speedy time limit, the game can last longer. Much longer.

Fressinet – Kosteniuk

Viljandy 2007

White to move

This occurred after 121 moves in a rapid tournament. Neither player was keeping score. White could have claimed a draw at Move 171 but did not have the scoresheet to prove it.

The game went on until Move 237, when White resigned because he was about to be mated. He had blundered on Move 228.

The 50-move rule is relatively modern and only gained widespread acceptance in the 1800s.

370. How old are other rules?

We don't know. They were created separately, over the centuries.

The way a rook moves has not changed in a millennium. But other rules were introduced in the last 500 years and varied from country to county.

For example, castling was once called the "king's leap." The rule we know was not standardized until the 19th century. Before then, there were games such as this:

NN – A. Severino

Naples 1723

1 e4 c5 2 ♘c3 e5 3 ♘f3 ♘c6 4 ♘d5 d6 5 c3 f5 6 exf5 ♗xf5 7 ♗b5 ♕d7 8 d4 cxd4 9 cxd4 0-0-0 10 ♘g1 ♔b8 11 ♘f3 ♖e8 12 dxe5 ♘xe5

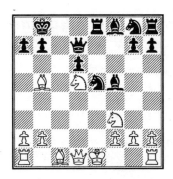

White to move

13 ♗xd7?? ♘xf3+ 14 ♔f1 ♗d3+ 15 ♕xd3 ♖e1 mate.

This is the bogus version of the game you will find in some databases.

What really happened is that Black did not castle by shifting his king to c8 and his rook to d8.

Instead, he played ...♔b8 in one move and ...♖e8 in the next. This was allowed as a "king's leap." The strange 10 ♘g1 and 11 ♘f3 have been added to conform to modern rules.

371. Why is there the en passant rule?

It closes a loophole.

In older rules of chess, a pawn could only advance one square, even on its first move.

The modern rule that allowed a two-square advance created the loophole. This permitted the pawn to evade the P-takes-P capture that would have been possible if it only moved one square.

This seemed unfair so en passant was created. The pawn could be captured "in passing" – "en passant" in French.

This was confusing at the time it was introduced and is still confusing to beginners. Some wrongly believe that if you do not exercise the right to capture en passant when it was first available you can do so later.

372. Who enforces the rules in a tournament?

An arbiter. In most cases, you have to appeal to him if you experience a breaking of the rules.

If the arbiter is not present at the time of the infraction, disputes often occur: "You touched your queen. You have to move it." ("Did not!" "Did too!")

373. What if I touch a piece accidentally while centering another piece on a square?

The tournament rule says touch-move only applies if you clearly intended to move. But make sure you say "J'adoube" first.

374. Are any rules optional?

Yes. If you and your opponent repeat the same positions four, five, ten times, the game is not automatically a draw. It goes on until someone claims a draw.

The same for the touch-move rule and 50-move draw rule.

375. If I don't claim a draw, do I still need to keep my scoresheet up to date?

You will if your opponent makes a claim and you want to dispute it.

Establishing whether the same position has occurred three times – with the same player to move each time – can be complex. An arbiter may need to examine both scoresheets to determine the truth.

376. What do I need to claim a draw due to insufficient mating material?

Just the position on the board. If your opponent has only his king and a bishop and you have just a king, it is obvious there is no possible position in which you would be mated.

But be careful. If he has just two knights and you have a king, there are ways you can lose by making a blunder.

Black to move

A draw claim would not be allowed. The reason is **1...♚h8?? 2 ♘f7** is mate.

The extreme form of insufficient mating material is "bare king." Under the pre-1500 rules, there was a second way to win a chess game: capture all of your opponent's pieces and pawns. This was called "bare king" and scored as a victory.

The rule disappeared long ago but you sometimes see modern players playing out a dead-drawn position until neither player has anything left.

377. Why?

Good question. Some players with an advantage play until the bitter end because they don't want to concede a draw. Others play on because they feel good about making every effort.

So – Carlen

Wijk aan Zee 2020

White to move

The two players could easily have agreed to a draw now. White made the outcome obvious with **50 ♖f3+** and **51 ♖xf4**.

But the game continued **51...♖xf4+ 54 ♔xf4** and only then was a draw affixed.

378. Can I promote to a queen if I still have my original queen?

André Philidor said "no" when he articulated the rules of the game as he knew them, more than two centuries ago. But today you can make a second queen or a third, fourth – or even a ninth.

In recent years, manufacturers of tournament-quality sets have included a second pair of queens, one White and one Black, to avoid situations like this:

Blackstock – Crouch

London 1980

1 c4 c6 2 ♘f3 d5 3 d4 ♘f6 4 ♘c3 e6 5 e3 ♘bd7 6 ♗d3 dxc4 7 ♗xc4 b5 8 ♗e2 ♗b7 9 e4 b4 10 e5 bxc3 11 exf6 cxb2 12 fxg7

Black to move

Here the game was stopped for 10 minutes – because Black wanted to play 12...bxa1(♛) – and White wanted to reply 13 gxh8(♛). But there were no extra queens to be used for the promotions.

There is a convention, but not a rule, that if you need to make a second queen, you can temporarily use an upside-down rook as a queen substitute.

379. Do rules ever conflict with one another?

They can and it may take an arbiter to resolve the conflict.

Suppose a player makes a move that prompts his opponent to resign. But it actually creates stalemate.

Is it a loss because of the resignation? Or is it a draw because of the position on the board?

An arbiter would say stalemate ends the game. What happens after does not matter.

380. Seems like there are a lot of rules. Do experienced players ever break one?

Even grandmasters do it unintentionally. Most violations are due to time trouble, such as when a player with only seconds left ignores a check. There have been several cases when elite players violate the castling rule because they forgot they had previously moved one of their castling pieces.

Illescas – Kamsky

Manila 1990

1 e4 c6 2 c4 d5 3 cxd5 cxd5 4 exd5 ♘f6 5 ♘c3 ♘xd5 6 ♘f3 g6 7 ♕b3 ♘b6 8 ♗b5+ ♗d7 9 ♘e5 e6 10 ♘e4 ♗e7 11 d4 ♗xb5 12 ♕xb5+ ♘8d7 13 ♗h6 a6 14 ♕e2 ♗b4+ 15 ♔f1 ♘d5 16 ♘xf7! ♔xf7 17 ♘g5+ ♔e8 18 ♕xe6+ ♕e7 19 ♕xd5

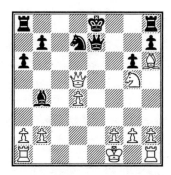

Black to move

Black knew he couldn't play 19...0-0 because g8 is attacked by White. But he tried to play 19...0-0-0. His opponent reminded him that he had moved his king. Black had to move his king. He lost after 19...♔d8.

And within two years he was among the world's 20 best players.

There are all sorts of additional rules and regulations, including relatively new ones governing on-line games. It is not worth studying the obscure rules to any great degree. There are more useful things to learn.

Chapter Eighteen: Winning a Won Game

381. Why do masters say, "Nothing is harder than winning a won game"?

Winning "technique," as it is called, is difficult to master because it requires skills very different from those used in the other phases of a game.

Instead of accumulating advantages, you need to exploit them. A bizarre case of that:

Deep Junior – Deep Fritz

Cafaques 2001

White to move

White chose **70 ♖c6+!** for a reason that makes perfect sense to a computer.

If Black captures the rook, the simplified position could be found in databases, which contain the best moves in all positions with five or less pieces and pawns.

White could then play the database moves and deliver mate in fewer than 30 moves.

Black had a database, too. It stayed out of database range with **70...♚b5!**.

Of course, there are more rational ways to win from the position in the diagram, or the one after 70...♚b5.

But the easiest was to force Black to accept the rook.

White did it with **71 ♖c5+ ♚b4 72 ♖b5+ ♚c4 73 ♖d4+ ♚c3 74 ♖c5+!**.

Black to move

White would meet 74...♔b3 with 75 ♖b4+ ♔a3 76 ♖a5+! ♖xa5.

This is another database position and White can mate in 32 moves.

Black chose **74...♔xd4** because it would then take White 35 moves to mate.

What Black was doing was what defenders normally do: Resist defeat as long as possible.

What White was doing is what we all do when trying to win a won game: Reduce the amount of thinking we have to do.

382. What does "a matter of technique" mean?

This is a cliché that players use to dismiss the position they are looking at.

They mean it is so favorable that it requires no more than routine measures to win. But unless you are a computer using your database, routine measures are rarely that routine.

383. How much more material do I need to gain in an ending to be sure of a win?

Often, none.

Technique is not about adding to the material you have already won. It is making that material advantage work for you.

White even used his extra rook that way in the diagram of Question 381.

384. But if I have two extra pawns, won't winning a third make victory much easier?

Easier, but not much easier.

A typical endgame textbook focuses on how to win with one extra pawn.

It devotes ten times as much space to it than to a two-pawn edge. The reason is that with a two-pawn edge you can win with much less effort or book knowledge.

But after a second pawn you run into another law of diminishing returns.

385. How so?

Each additional pawn increases the winning chances marginally.

Consider the situation with one extra pawn:

White to move

White's winning chances are scant.

He cannot win the g6-pawn unless Black blunders very badly. That means White has to create a passed pawn and try to promote it. But Black's king can easily blockade it.

However, with another White pawn, the situation changes dramatically.

386. Why?

Then he will likely create two passed pawns. It may be impossible for Black's king to blockade both of them.

If we add a White pawn, say to h4, in the last diagram, his advantage grows to more than +9, in computer evaluations.

Then it truly is a "matter of technique."

387. Where is the diminishing return?

You can see it when we add another White pawn, say to e3.

White wins easily

White does not need three passed pawns to win.

With the best moves being played by both players, he might shorten the game by several moves, compared to the position with two extra pawns.

However, the outcome would not be in doubt. The computer evaluation grows, but only to +10.

Remember, the goal of proper technique is to make winning easier. In some cases, this is done by giving up some of your extra material.

388. How can that be?

Because the easiest way to win is usually to promote a pawn.

If it is difficult to create a passed pawn through normal means, your best winning chance may lie in surrendering material.

McShane – Baburin

Kilkenny 1994

Black to move

White's rook cannot capture the bishop or force mate. Yet Black resigned. Why?

The answer is, White can give up the Exchange to win at least one pawn, with 54.♖d7+, 55.♔c6, 56 ♖b7 and 57 ♖xb6!. Then the win is trivially easy.

389. Are there basic priorities of good technique?

Yes. High on the list is denying counterplay.

In positions with few pieces, like the last diagram, stifling counterplay is elementary. Here is a slightly more challenging "matter of technique."

Tiviakov – Janssen

Leeuwarden 2003

White to move

The win would be difficult, if not impossible, after 56 ♔c3 ♗g1!.

But **56 ♘c3+! ♔b6 57 ♘e2!** imprisoned the Black bishop.

This reduced the struggle to a mismatch: White's king and b-pawn versus Black's king. There is zero counterplay.

Once White had made sufficient progress with his passed pawn, he could free his knight.

Black resigned after **57...♔b5 58 ♔c3 ♔b6 59 ♔c4 ♔c6 60 b5+ ♔b6 61 ♔b4 ♔b7 62 ♔a5 ♔a7 63 b6+ ♔b7 64 ♔b5 ♔b8 65 ♔a6.**

White would have played ♘d4-c6 and threatened b7 mate.

390. Suppose I see a way that seems to make winning certain. Should I look for a faster way?

This is good thinking – in a middlegame.

That is when the maxim "If you see a good move, look for a better one" serves well. If you find a stronger move, it may shorten the game.

But shortening the game is not a high priority in an endgame. Remember the mantra "Don't hurry."

Instead, there is a practical rule cited by Paul Keres: Don't look for a second winning continuation once you are certain of the first.

You can only win a game once. That was a favorite saying of a colleague of Keres, who wasn't known for his technique: Mikhail Tal. Whether you prompt resignation in ten moves or 30, you still score only one point.

391. My technique is awful. How can I improve it?

One of the best ways to train your technique is to play against a computer. Set up an endgame with what should be a winning material edge, such as with the three extra pawns in Question 387.

Play it out against the best resistance the computer can muster. Once you can do that comfortably, try it with two extra pawns.

A more advanced method is to start at the very end of a master game. Take the final positions from games won by your favorite player.

After his opponent resigned, continue the game, letting the computer play the moves of the player who resigned. Try to finish the game, ending with mate.

392. Is there a proper attitude for good technique?

Tell yourself, "I'm winning. This is going to take time."

393. OK, what is the wrong attitude?

One is thinking that the position will win itself. Another is to feel upset that your opponent is playing on in a position that seems so easily won.

Bent Larsen, one of the greatest endgame players, said "lack of patience" is probably the most common reason for not winning a won game.

394. But what if I have four extra pawns and he still won't resign?

Make four queens.

Chapter Nineteen: Training

395. What is chess training?

Training includes everything that can prepare you to play at your best.

It means studying but also physical exercise, playing practice games, being well rested and so on.

Mikhail Botvinnik devised a personal training method that helped make him the world's best player. His regimen included taking a nap before a round and how he walked to the tournament site. (Take the same route at the same time every round, he said.)

396. Should I play more than I study?

That's the big question. Grandmasters have tried to answer it in precise terms. Their answers are all over the map.

Pal Benko, a world-class player, recommended spending 75 percent of your chess time on studying, 25 percent on playing.

Another grandmaster, Mato Damjanović, said 80 percent playing and 20 percent studying was the right balance. A third GM, Eugenio Torre, said 65 percent studying, and so on.

In other words, there is no right answer. Find what works for you.

397. Can someone become a good player with just book study?

Better than good.

Vasily Smyslov's father had a huge chess library. Young Vasily did not play someone outside his family until he visited a park at age 15. Soon after that his first published game appeared:

Gerasimov – Smyslov

Moscow 1935

1 d4 d5 2 ♘f3 ♘f6 3 e3 e6 4 ♗d3 c5 5 b3 ♘c6 6 ♗b2 ♗d6 7 0-0 ♕c7 8 a3 b6 9 c4 ♗b7 10 ♘c3 a6 11 ♖e1 cxd4 12 exd4 0-0 13 ♘a4 ♗f4

14 ♘e5? dxc4! 15 bxc4 ♘xe5 16 dxe5 ♕c6! 17 ♗f1 ♖fd8 18 ♕b3? ♘g4! 19 h3

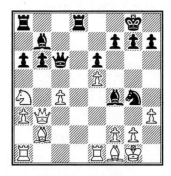

Black to move

After **19...♖d3!**, Black would win quickly following 20 ♗xd3 ♕xg2 mate or 20 ♕xd3 ♗h2+ 21 ♔h1 ♘xf2+ 22 ♔xh2 ♘xd3.

The game ended with **20 ♕xb6 ♖xh3! 21 ♗d4 ♗h2+ 22 ♔h1 ♗xe5+**.

White resigned in view of 23 ♔g1 ♗h2+ 24 ♔g1 ♗c7+ and ...♗xb6. Smyslov was soon recognized as a potential champion.

398. What about the opposite – just playing a lot?

Several great players said they rarely looked at a chess book before they were masters. "I was never a student," said Yasser Seirawan. "I learned only by playing, and mainly by five-minute games."

Anatoly Karpov said he began to take chess seriously when he played fellow schoolboys in the courtyard of his apartment building. He estimated that he played about 1,000 games in less than six months.

He quickly progressed. Here he is at 10 years old, playing a board in a simultaneous exhibition against the man who became one of his greatest rivals.

Korchnoi – Karpov

Zlatoust 1961

1 e4 e5 2 ♘f3 ♘c6 3 d4 exd4 4 ♘xd4 ♘f6 5 ♘c3 d6 6 ♗b5 ♗d7 7 0-0 ♗e7 8 ♖e1 0-0 9 ♗f1 ♖e8 10 h3 ♘xd4 11 ♕xd4 ♗c6 12 ♗e3 ♕d7 13 ♖ad1 ♗f8 14 ♗g5 ♗e7 15 ♗c1 a6 16 g4 h6 17 f4 ♖ad8 18 ♗g2 ♕c8 19 ♕d3 b5 20 a3 ♕b7 21 ♕f3 ♗f8 22 h4 a5 23 g5 hxg5 24 hxg5 ♘h7 25 ♗h3

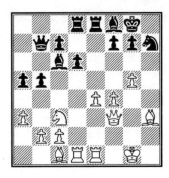

Black to move

White's kingside attack would be overwhelming if 26 ♘d5! and 27 g6 are allowed.

25...d5! 26 exd5 ♖xe1+ 27 ♖xe1 ♗xd5 28 ♘xd5 ♕xd5 29 ♕xd5 ♖xd5 30 g6 ♗c5+ draw

White would still be better after 31 ♔f1! ♘f8, but not by much.

399. How did great players make the choice between playing more and studying more?

Personality and opportunity had a lot to do with it.

Reuben Fine found school so easy that he had plenty of free time for chess. There were few good books when he was growing up. Instead of studying, he spent several hours a day, several days a week, playing at the Marshall Chess Club.

If Fine or Karpov had had a teacher, they might have studied more. But again, personality plays a role.

Jack Collins served as a mentor to two brothers, Robert and Donald Byrne. The Byrnes had the same upbringing and schooling, the same amount of free time, the same opportunities to play and study.

Robert turned out to be a book fanatic. Donald played rather than read. They turned out to be equally great players.

400. Are there stages of getting better?

Several. Here's one way of looking at them:

The beginner knows little more than how the pieces move. The *post-beginner* develops his first criteria for selecting a move. They may be naïve – "I like knight moves because it surprises my opponent," for example. But having any criteria is a big first step.

The next level is that of the *novice*. He has learned general principles. But he still wins most games by capturing pieces left en prise by his opponent.

By the time he is an *improving amateur,* he can recognize most enemy threats. He has begun to analyze and evaluate candidate moves.

The *experienced tournament player* is much stronger because he has a more sophisticated way of choosing moves. He has developed an intuitive sense of good moves but knows he has to carefully calculate them.

The *master* can play good moves instantly. He relies on intuition, not calculation, more than non-masters.

There are other, more personal milestones in a player's chess education. One is when you can survive well into the middlegame when playing a worthy opponent.

"I became a good player when I started losing well," Seirawan recalled. "The games weren't just a wipeout."

401. I hear intuition mentioned a lot. What is chess intuition exactly?

Herbert Simon, a prize-winning economist/psychologist – and also a serious tournament player – said in general intuition "is nothing more and nothing less than recognition."

In chess, it is recognizing patterns and ideas that you've seen previously. This is how masters are able to make instant decisions in positions that would take non-masters hours to decipher.

The more developed a player's intuition is, the greater his ability to detect a good but unusual move.

Wojtaszek – Caruana

Wijk aan Zee 2021

Black to move

Fellow grandmasters were mystified by **13...♗xc3!**.

It not only violated general principles – this was a very good bishop – but was unlike good moves in previous grandmaster games. It was counter-intuitive.

"If this is good for Black, I need to learn chess again," Grandmaster Ivan Sokolov said.

Fabiano Caruana said after the game he wasn't sure ...♗xc3 was correct. "But I had seen some *similar* examples where White can't really free himself."

The benefits became clear after **14 ♕xc3 ♕f6 15 ♕c1 ♘c5** because defending the e4-pawn was a problem for White.

Caruana pocketed a pawn after **16 ♕b1 ♕e6 17 ♖fe1 ♕xc4** and soon won.

402. What other skill is important to acquire?

Quick sight. This is the ability to look at a position for the first time and take little time to spot all the potential tactics.

With quick sight you see all the possible captures and checks that either player can make.

403. How do I acquire quick sight?

You can practice by looking at random positions from one of the many Web sites that cover recent games.

Click on a game, then find a middlegame position, say after 20 or 30 moves have been played. Size it up as quickly as you can, and try to answer questions:

Is any piece or pawn unprotected? Can it be captured? What is the material situation? Is there a tactic that is threatened?

You should also take notice of knight moves because opponents are most likely to overlook them. "The weaker the player, the more terrible the knight is to him," Capablanca said.

404. Is quick sight the same as calculating ability?

No, the two are different. Quick sight is the ability to spot a tactical idea. Calculating is working out the consequences of that idea.

Here is how the world's two best players of a previous era confused their fans:

Kasparov – Karpov

Linares 1994

Black to move

Black played **13...a4.**

After the game, spectators wanted to know why he avoided 13...♝xa3 – and why White allowed it.

The fans had seen 14 ♖xa3? ♕xc1+. That was the easy part.

They had also concluded Black would be much better after 14 bxc3 ♕c3+.

But the position is more complex because of 14 ♝xh6!. Evaluating this takes calculation.

Yet neither player got that far. Neither had seen 13...♝xa3!. Their quick sight had failed.

405. Is there a way to train my chess memory?

There's no magical method to remember 20 moves of opening analysis, if that's what you have in mind.

Some players have developed a generally good memory which somehow allowed them to absorb chess information.

Garry Kasparov was asked how he trained his memory. He said he didn't:

"The only time, if you can call it training, was when I was 12 to 14. Mama always asked me to learn by heart some poem of Pushkin or Lermontov. It was her form of repetition."

Masters often deplore memorizing but then they extol pattern recognition – which is based largely on rote learning.

406. If I play training games, should it be with players my own strength? Or should it be with players I know I can beat?

Neither. You will learn more by playing opponents slightly stronger than you.

You may lose most of the time. But you should be competitive in the games.

The guideline is "Train hard, fight easy." This is a military motto but it applies to chess.

It also works with physical conditioning. Many would-be athletes train themselves by lifting heavier weights, running longer distances and otherwise exerting themselves in more intense ways than they would in a competition.

Chess players do the same when they play better opponents or choose a faster or longer time limit.

407. How fast?

If you want to play in a tournament with a rapid time limit, such as 25 minutes for the entire game, try playing games with a 20-minute limit.

This will pressure you to make quicker decisions. When you enter the tournament, 25 minutes may seem like a luxury.

On the other hand, before playing at a slower time limit you want to strengthen your stamina, not your speed.

Mikhail Tal made a training blunder after he underwent a serious medical operation. He played practice games while he recovered. But he made sure they would not exhaust him. They were limited to three hours, instead of the five hours he would see in an upcoming tournament.

He did well in the training games and convinced himself he was thinking well. But when the tournament began he tired in the fourth hour and blundered in the fifth.

Tal – Filip

Curacao 1962

1 e4 c5 2 ♘f3 e6 3 d4 cxd4 4 ♘xd4 a6 5 ♘c3 ♕c7 6 f4 b5 7 a3 ♗b7 8 ♕f3 ♘f6 9 ♗d3 ♗c5 10 ♘b3 ♗e7 11 0-0 0-0 12 ♗d2 d6 13 g4 d5 14 e5 ♘fd7 15 ♕h3 g6 16 ♘d4 ♘c6 17 ♘ce2 ♘xd4 18 ♘xd4 ♘c5 19 b4! ♘e4 20 ♗e3 ♖fe8 21 ♖ae1 ♗f8 22 ♘f3 a5 23 f5! exf5 24 gxf5 ♖xe5

White to move

Tal could have finished off a well-played game with 25 ♘xe5 ♕xe5 26 c3! and ♗d4. But he began to drift:

25 fxg6? hxg6 26 ♘xe5 ♕xe5 27 c3 axb4 28 ♗d4 ♗c8! 29 ♕g2? ♕h5 30 ♗xe4 dxe4 31 ♕xe4? ♕g5+ 32 ♔h1 ♗e6 33 ♗e5 ♖d8 34 h4 ♕h5 35 ♕f4 ♖d3 36 ♗f6 ♕d5+ 37 ♔g1 bxc3 38 ♖e4 ♗c5+ 39 ♔h2 ♕a2+ White resigns.

Tal's stamina gave out and he couldn't use one of his greatest strengths: his ability to calculate. He should have trained by playing six-hour games.

You may also benefit by planning your study sessions for the same length as a tournament game.

408. Why?

Same reasoning. If you want to feel comfortable in a four-hour game, it pays to study for four hours straight. This was one of Viktor Korchnoi's training tricks.

And, by the way, some masters prefer to look at a game using a real board and real pieces, even today.

Experienced teachers say that computer-trained players often have difficulty playing on a physical board, in a face-to-face tournament, after training with a computer screen.

409. If I want to take training seriously, is there anything else I should consider?

Several great players of the past spoke highly of playing correspondence chess. This was conducted by snail mail. Games could take a year to finish.

But each time a move arrived on a postcard, it was a new lesson. They were emotionally interested in finding the best move. If that meant they had to open up an opening book and study alternative variations, it was something they felt highly motivated to do.

Keres – Faltweber

Correspondence 1932

1 ♘f3 d5 2 e4? dxe4 3 ♘g5 ♗f5 4 ♘c3 ♘f6 5 ♗c4 e6 6 f3! exf3 7 ♕xf3

Black to move

Now 7...♗g6 is fine for Black (8 ♕xb7 ♘bd7).

7...c6 8 ♘xf7! ♚xf7 9 ♕xf5 ♕e7 10 ♘e4 h6 11 ♘c5 g6 12 ♕xe6+ ♚e8 13 0-0 b5 14 ♕c8+ ♕d8 15 ♖e1+ ♗e7 16 ♖xe7+! ♚xe7 17 ♕e6+ ♚f8 18 ♕f7 mate.

Today you can play a form of correspondence chess on turn-based Web sites. Allow yourself plenty of time for each move, say a day or more. Remember: Motivated studying is quality studying.

Chapter Twenty: **Technical Terms**

410. *I see all sorts of technical terms in books and on the Internet. How many of them do I need to know?*

You can safely forget many, if not most, of them.

You will never need to identify the Arabian mate, for example. No one is going to ask you to describe Alekhine's gun.

When we talked about the technical terms for tactics (Question 62), we saw how the ideas are useful but the names are not important. Other terms can just be confusing.

Whoever moves loses

For obscure reasons, this is called a *trebuchet*, the French word for "catapult."

This is also called "knight opposition" because the kings are a knight's move away from one another. Neither term is particularly helpful.

And it also called "mutual zugzwang." That is, a true zugzwang (Question 291) because whoever has to move would lose.

For example, 1 ♔g4 ♔xe4 if it's White's turn. And 1...♔d3 2 ♔xe5 if it is Black's.

The zugzwang *idea* is worth remembering. But the names for the position aren't.

There are other technical terms that are used so casually they have almost lost meaning.

411. Such as?

Such as "classical." It can mean a style of play, a group of center pawns or a time limit or be part of an opening name.

Or take something as simple as "the center." Masters talk about controlling it, giving it up, and so on.

But do they mean the four squares e4, d4, e5 and d5? Sometimes.

Yet, at other times they may be talking about the larger center of 16 squares, from f3 to f5 to c5 to c3. And if a king has not yet castled it can be still "in the center," at e1 or e8.

412. What should I do when I encounter a new term?

Before you look it up on the Internet, try to figure it out by using common sense. Then you may remember it better.

"Centralize" sounds deep. But it just means to move pieces towards the center, however you define the center.

"To liquidate" means to trade material and defuse pawn tension.

"To consolidate" means to reorganize your pieces so they cooperate better with one another. This often happens when they lose some coordination after winning material.

A "miniature" is a short game, usually 20 or fewer moves. Also known as a brevity.

The "text move" is the move that was played in the game being analyzed.

"Castling by hand" means, for example, getting White's king to g1 by moving it twice, rather than by 0-0.

A "flight square" is an escape route for a piece that comes under attack.

A "spite check" is a check given in a lost position, for the sake of making one last forcing move. Better to have checked and lost than never to have checked at all.

413. How old are these terms?

Many are no more than a century old. But the ideas they describe are much older.

"To double rooks" was accepted as a technical term around 1800. The idea that doubling rooks on the seventh rank is strong dates back at least to the 10th century.

414. What terms relate to attacking the king?

A "king hunt" occurs after a king is driven from its haven, either at e1 or e8 in the opening or in a castled position. It may take several moves until the king is cornered.

A "pawn storm" is the use of two or more pawns to open up a castled king position.

"Castling into it" occurs when a king has become more vulnerable after castling.

Mengarini – Ervin

Lone Pine 1971

Black to move

After **9...0-0** Black was doomed by **10 ♗d3!**.

There was no defense to 11 h4! and 12 ♘g5, with its threat of ♕xh7 mate.

Black resigned after **11...♗d7 11 h4** in view of 11...♗e8 12 ♘g5 ♗xg5 13 hxg5 or 12...h6 13 ♘gxe6!.

The losing move, it turned out, was 9...0-0??.

415. Are there any pawn terms I may not have heard?

Aron Nimzovich popularized "attack on the base of the pawn chain." This means to try to chip away at the last pawn in a chain, so the more advanced pawns become vulnerable.

For example, after **1 e4 e6 2 d4 d5 3 e5,** the move **3...c5** attacks the base of the chain of d4- and e5-pawns. If the c5-pawn is traded for the d4-pawn, the e5-pawn loses its support.

When pawns are exchanged, some of them can be separated from the others by one file or more. You can speak of each group as a "pawn island."

Pawn Islands

White's pawns are separated into three islands and Black's are separated into two. Generally, the more islands you have, the more likely some of the pawns are going to be weak.

This diagram also illustrates another technical term, *luft*.

It's a German word ("air") that means pushing a pawn in front of your castled king so that you won't be mated by a rook or queen check on the first rank. White's king has the flight square of h2 and Black has g7.

If there are no rooks or queens on the board, no first-rank checks are possible and luft has no special relevance.

416. What about terms related to strategy?

To "give up the center" means you make a pawn-takes-pawn capture that leaves your opponent with more pawns on the four center squares than you do.

For example, if Black has pawns on e5 and d6 and White had pawns on e4 and d4, the capture ...exd4 by Black gives up the center.

Nimzovich was fond of "overprotection." He meant to guard a center square with more pieces than necessary.

A "minority attack" is an attempt to weaken an opponent's pawn majority, typically on the queenside.

If a strategic plan succeeds, it can create a "bind."

417. And that is?

A bind is a powerful grip on the position. A player who enjoys a bind can take his time finishing off because his opponent lacks counterplay. In this position White has a bind.

Tarrasch – Walbrodt

Berlin 1898

White to move

His best winning plan is h4-h5, followed by hxg6 and eventually ♗e2-h5.

It's an elaborate plan, but Black cannot stop it.

But White waited. His bind was so strong that he had time to improve his endgame chances by centralizing his king with **43 ♔g3 ♗e8 44 ♔f4**.

The rest was **44...♗d7 45 h5! ♗e8 46 hxg6 ♗xg6 47 ♗e2! ♕d8 48 ♗h5! ♗xh5 49 ♕xh5 ♖xg5 50 ♖xg5 ♖xg5 51 ♕xg5 ♕f8 52 e6 resigns**.

Thanks to his improved king position, White would have won the pawn endgame after 51...♕xg5+ 52 ♔xg5.

418. That brings up endgame terms. Are there rare ones I should know?

"Triangulation" is a way of moving the king in a triangle in order to lose a move.

This is best explained in a position like this.

White to play and win

White's best winning idea is to bring his king around to the right, ♔c3-d3-e4-d5.

But 1 ♔c3? fails because of 1...♚a4 2 ♔d3 ♚b4! and White has to be careful to avoid losing.

Now imagine that it was Black's turn to move in the diagram.

He would lose after 1...♚b6 2 ♔c3 ♚a5 and now 3 ♔d2!.

The point is that 3...♚b4 4 ♔d3 puts Black in zugzwang. White's king has moved in a triangle, c3-d2-d3.

The way White can win in the diagram is **1 ♔a3! ♚b6 2 ♔a4 ♚a6 3 ♔a3.**

Then **3...♚a5 4 ♔b3!** puts Black in zugzwang.

And 3...♚b6 4 ♔c2! triangulates again.

Black to move

Black loses after 4...♚a5 5 ♔d2 ♚a4 6 ♔e3 ♚a3 7 ♔e4.

419. Are there opening terms I should know?

There are some you should at least be aware of.

The "fork trick" is a simple combination to gain a superior pawn center. A common version of it is **1 e4 e5 2 ♘f3 ♘c6 3 ♘c3 ♗c5?** and now

White to move

4 ♘xe5! ♘xe5 5 d4.

White has the better of 5…♗xd4 6 ♕xd4 or 4…♗xf2+ 5 ♔xf2 ♘xe5 6 d4!.

A "battle of the tempo" is a situation in which neither player wants to make a committal move.

This term was often used when games began with the Queen's Gambit Declined: **1 d4 d5 2 c4 e6 3 ♘c3 ♘f6 4 ♗g5 ♗e7 5 e3 0-0 6 ♘f3 ♘bd7 7 ♖c1 c6**.

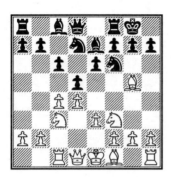

White to move

One of Black's standard ideas is an exchange of pieces after …dxc4, followed by … ♘d5. For example, 8 ♗d3 dxc4 9 ♗xc4 ♘d5.

If, however, White inserts a useful move, 8 ♕c2, then 8…dxc4 9 ♗xc4 ♘d5 helps him. He saved a tempo by not playing ♗d3.

Therefore, Black can try to insert his own useful move, such as 8…♖e8 or 8…a6. Then on 9 ♗d3 dxc4! he has won the "battle of the tempo." White can avoid this with another useful move, 9 a3, and the waiting game goes on.

420. This is a lot to remember. Are there any terms I must know?

You probably know them already.

En prise means that something is capable of being captured ("He put his knight en prise").

You will hear "swindle" to mean an unwarranted victory ("I was winning easily but he swindled me").

421. One final question. Why did my last opponent call me a fish?

He was insulting you. Chess has a rich vocabulary for weak players and moves. A fish or *patzer* plays *lemons* and *hangs* his pieces.

That is, he makes inferior moves and loses unprotected pieces.

A duffer, or "weakie" as Bobby Fischer would call a much lower-rated player, may also play the first aggressive move that occurs to him. "Patzer sees a check, patzer gives a check," as kibitzers say about a novice.

Or he may fall for a *cheapo*. This is a move that "threatens something so obvious that only an idiot would fall for it, and he does," wrote a master – and professional psychologist – Eliot Hearst.

Chapter Twenty One: Strategy

422. How is strategy different from tactics?

Strategy is essentially the making of plans.

It is based on visualizing a future position – looking ahead without considering your opponent's moves.

In contrast, tactics requires calculating – looking ahead but carefully weighing your opponent's replies.

423. Can I win a game without making a plan?

You make simple plans all the time without knowing it.

Pushing a passed pawn with the intent of queening is a plan.

Whenever you mate with a king and rook against a king, you are using a series of simple plans.

White to move

White's first plan is to restrict the king. It is accomplished by **1 ♖h5!**.

The second plan is to get White's king close to the Black king. For example, **1...♚d6 2 ♔e2 ♚c6 3 ♔d3 ♚d6 4 ♔e4**.

The next plan is to force the king back, **4...♚e6 5 ♖h6+**.

Or after **4...♚c6 5 ♔d4 ♚b6 6 ♔c4 ♚a6 7 ♔b4 ♚b6 8 ♖h6+**.

This is followed by repeating the process on the next rank, and so on.

424. But don't masters claim they make much deeper plans?

Yes but they are also masters of exaggeration. When they annotate their games they can make it appear their winning plan began with 1 d4.

There is an oft-quoted statement by a great teacher, Evgeny Znosko-Borovsky, that goes: "It is not a move, even the best move, that you must seek, but a realizable plan."

Today we know the best players can beat us by doing the opposite: They are computers. They seek the best move. But they cannot plan, at least in the way we do.

425. Has strategy become more important as chess has evolved?

In a way, it has become less important. Masters used to emphasize long-range planning much more.

Under the pre-1500 rules of chess, the rival armies often did not come into contact with one another in the first ten moves. Tactics were not possible until well after each side had made strategic decisions.

Perhaps the oldest recorded game, Assuli – Al Lajlaj from the tenth century, began **1 f3 f6 2 f4** (Pawns could only advance one square).

White chose a strategy based on concentrating his most powerful pieces – his rook and knight – on the kingside, with ♘f3, ♖g1 and a coordinated advance of his g-pawn.

Black opted for the same strategy: **2...f5 3 ♘f3 ♘f6 4 g3 g6 5 ♖g1 ♖g8 6 h3 h6 7 e3 e6**.

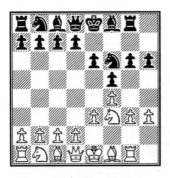

White to move

The symmetry continued after **8 g4 fxg4 9 hxg4 g5 10 fxg5 hxg5 11 d3 d6**, until the tactics began.

426. How long does a master's plan last?

Most plans last two to four moves. There are too many tactical factors to allow longer plans to succeed.

Plans are often just an idea based on a threat that becomes apparent in a few moves.

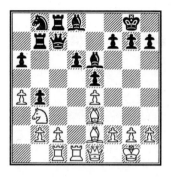

Tseshkovsky – Novikov

Yerevan 1984

White to move

White chose **18 ♘d2!**. His goal was to play ♘c4xd6, a three-move plan.

Black managed to avert the threat to his d-pawn, with **18...♕c6 19 b3 ♘d7? 20 ♘c4 ♗c7**.

But he should have played more actively. He had given White a free hand to begin a second plan.

This plan is aimed at embarrassing Black's queen after an opening of the c-file, with **21 c3!**.

Black to move

Following 21...bxc3 22 ♖xc3, Black would have no good answer to threats such as 23 ♘a5.

Instead, he tried **21...♘c5 22 cxb4 ♘xb3** and resigned soon after **23 ♘a5 ♕xe4 24 ♗f3 ♕xb4 25 ♗xb7**.

427. Is that what happens in a master game – one good plan is followed by another?

That's what happens in a model game. It usually takes a few different plans, each lasting only a few moves, to create a significant advantage.

But most plans fail, not because they were badly conceived but because the opposing player anticipated them.

428. How should I evaluate a plan?

A good plan seeks a substantial and realizable goal. It should do more than look constructive.

Here is how a poor plan was famously bested by a good plan.

Spassky – Fischer

World Championship match 1972

White to move

White chose the logical-looking maneuver **18 ♖b2** and **19 ♖bf2**.

It was easy to accomplish and looked good when it happened.

But there was no work for the doubled rooks to do on the f-file. Black had a growing advantage after **18...♖b8 19 ♖bf2 ♕e7 20 ♗c2**.

The main difference was he had a plan of his own – **20...g5!** followed by ...♕e8-g6 and ...♘h5-f4. That would generate significant kingside pressure.

The game became famous because of a blunder. But it was strategically decided well before:

21 ♗d2 ♕e8 22 ♗e1 ♕g6 23 ♕d3 ♘h5 24 ♖xf8+ ♖xf8 25 ♖xf8+ ♔xf8 26 ♗d1 ♘f4 27 ♕c2?? ♗xa4 White resigns.

429. Is a maneuver a plan?

It often is. The maneuver 18 ♘d2! and 20 ♘c4 in Question 427 was a plan.

But a good plan is usually more than a shift of a piece from one square to another. It may involve an irrevocable change in the position, such as 21 c3! in that example or 20…g5! in the last example.

An irrevocable change would be a trade of pieces or pawns or just the advance of a pawn. Pawns can't move backward so they can't be said to maneuver.

430. Are pawns a big deal in strategy?

Very much so. One of the oldest surviving games, probably composed, went this way:

NN – Greco

Rome 1620

1 e4 e6 2 d4 d5 3 e5 c5 4 c3 ♘c6 5 ♘f3 ♗d7 6 ♗e3 c4 7 b3 b5!

White to move

Black's strategy was simply to expand on the queenside and deny White's pieces any good squares on that wing.

White found a good counter-strategy using pawns, **8 a4!** and then **8…a6 9 axb5 axb5 10 ♖xa8 ♕xa8**.

This eliminated most of Black's advantage in queenside space. Then **11 bxc4 dxc4!** inspired Black to find another plan, occupying d5 with a knight.

He eventually won after **12 ♗e2 ♘ge7 13 0-0 ♘d5 14 ♗d2 ♗e7 15 ♘g5 ♗xg5 16 ♗xg5 0-0 17 ♗f3 ♘a5 18 ♗xd5 ♕xd5 19 f4 ♗c6!**.

431. What are the ingredients of a good plan?

That depends on the goal.

If the aim is a mating attack, the ingredients are typically the concentration of your pieces in the target area, the opening of ranks or diagonals leading to that area and the rapid exploitation of a breach in the defense.

If the aim is more positional, the ingredients can be centralization, occupying outposts, seizing control of open lines for your bishops and rooks, mobilizing a pawn majority, creating a passed pawn, trading inferior pieces for better ones, gaining space – in short, all of the ways you can create or enhance a positional advantage.

432. How do I gain space?

Pushing pawns is the usual manner. The pawn structure determines who has more room for his pieces to operate safely.

Even though White makes the first move of a game he can begin the middlegame with less space, as the example in Question 162 showed. When you advance a pawn you may be adding to that space.

There are also rarer examples when a center with few or no pawns is occupied by minor pieces. This too can be considered a space advantage.

433. Is it possible to have too much space?

Yes, you can become over-extended. This means you don't have enough pieces to control the terrain you have seized.

Exploiting an over-extended opponent was one of the hallmarks of Hypermodern strategy.

Euwe – Rubinstein

The Hague 1921

1 e4 c5 2 ♘f3 ♘f6 3 e5 ♘d5 4 d4 cxd4 5 ♕xd4 e6 6 c4 ♘c6 7 ♕d1 ♘de7 8 ♗d2 ♘g6 9 ♕e2 ♕c7 10 ♗c3 b6 11 h4 d6! 12 exd6 ♗xd6 13 ♘bd2 ♘f4 14 ♕e3 ♗c5 15 ♕e4 f5! 16 ♕c2 0-0 17 g3 ♘g6 18 h5 ♘ge5 19 ♘xe5 ♘xe5

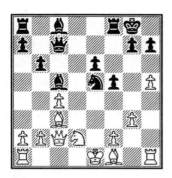

White to move

White gained space with 6 c4 but his greater control of terrain has vanished. He would be worse after 20 ♗g2 ♗b7 because he has too much space to defend.

20 b4? ♗xf2+! 21 ♔xf2 ♘g4+ 22 ♔e2 ♕xg3 (22...♗b7! 23 ♖g1 f4 wins) **23 ♗d4 ♗b7 24 ♖h3 ♕d6 25 ♕c3 e5 26 ♗g1 f4 27 c5 ♕h6 28 ♔e1 e4 29 ♖h4 ♕g5 30 ♕h3 ♘e3 31 ♗xe3 fxe3 32 ♗c4+ ♔h8 33 ♘f1 ♕f6 White resigns**

434. Which strategic principles are important to understand?

One is the Principle of Second Weakness.

You may be stopped when you attack an opponent's weakest spot. To make progress, you can switch to a second target.

We saw this when we talked about endgames (Question 309). It is also a major factor in middlegames.

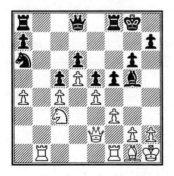

Petrosian – Simagin

Moscow 1956

White to move

White's strategy for the past 10 moves was to open and exploit the b-file. But he realized that 22 ♖b7 f4 and ...♘b4 soon reaches a dead end.

He began a new plan with **22 exf5!**.

Then 22...♖xf5 would surrender e4 to White's under-used knight.

But **22...gxf5 23 g4!** also secured e4 and created chances on the g-file as well. White was even willing to sacrifice a pawn, **23...fxg4 24 ♘e4!**, because of his kingside chances after 24...gxf3 25 ♖xf3 and ♗e3.

Black to move

Black abandoned the ...♘b4 idea but his knight could not defend his king.

Next came **25...♗f4 25. ♖b7 ♘c7 26 fxg4 ♘e8 27 g5 ♕c8 28 ♖e7 ♕h3 29 ♖f3 ♕g4 30 ♕d3**.

White's queen and two minor pieces outdueled Black's queen and rook following...

30...♗xh2 31 ♖xf8+ ♔xf8 32 ♖xe8+ ♖xe8 33 ♗xh2.

435. Should I always have a plan?

Not always. If you have a good move, you don't have to think further.

436. If planning is so important, why can't computers do it?

They don't think like us. Or, as programming pioneer Ken Thompson put it, "The question is not whether machines can think – but whether playing chess requires thinking."

Chapter Twenty Two: Practical Matters

437. I get nervous during games. What can I do?

Every player occasionally suffers from nerves during a game. Typical causes are fear of making the wrong move and anxiety due to a shortness of clock time.

Masters suffer from this too, but they are also masters of calming themselves down. "Nerves are merely a lack of confidence in your own ability," said Grandmaster John Fedorowicz.

438. How do I avoid getting short of time?

Think faster. But you already knew that.

The natural remedy is to stop searching for the absolutely best move in a position. If you found a move you know is good, it may be good enough.

You can train yourself to think this way by playing practice games. If the control is, say, 40 moves in 90 minutes, try to play your first 15 moves in no more than 30 minutes. If you are using a scoresheet, draw a line under the space for move 15 to remind yourself.

439. What should I do when my opponent gets into time trouble?

There are two schools of thought. One school says you should ignore his clock. Tell yourself: "Only the position matters."

Thinking about his lack of time can impair your judgment. You may be tempted to make second-best moves just to set traps or to complicate the position. Worse, you can allow his time shortage to make *you* nervous.

440. What is the other school of thought?

"Play the man, not the board," as in Question 352.

This means choosing moves that will either make your opponent's time pressure worse or exploit his inability to think as calmly as he would with more time.

Inexperienced players think they should make threats when their opponent is in time trouble. This can actually help him greatly. Instead of considering several candidate moves, he has to look only at the ones that defend. A better policy is to make solid but non-forcing moves (Question 48).

An alternative is to make moves that are neither good nor bad, just confusing.

Y. Grünfeld – Hug

Munich 1987

White to move

With two moves to reach the time control, White saw that 39 ♘xd5! might get no more than a draw after 39...♘xd5 40 ♕xd5 ♖e1+.

Instead, he chose the objectively inferior **39 ♔f1?**.

After **39...♔h8** he played **40 ♖e1**.

This didn't help him on the board. But it got Black wondering whether he could safely play 40...♖e4, so that 41 ♕xb6 d4.

The answer is yes (42 ♘c4? ♘d3 wins). But while he was calculating this his flag fell.

441. If my opponent is not in time trouble, what should I be doing when it is his turn to move?

If you are playing an over-the-board game, some masters would suggest getting up and taking a walk around the room. This can relieve stress. Others say you should never waste time that could be spent thinking at the board.

Simon Webb, in *Chess for Tigers,* offered this:

If your opponent is a time-pressure addict, "Walk away from the board and stay away so as not to wake him up."

442. What should I do if I realize I just made a blunder?

There is nothing much you can do in an online game. But if it is a face-to-face game, make yours a poker face. Don't give your opponent a clue.

Boris Spassky was famous for his deadpan expressions, regardless of what was happening on the board. But Bent Larsen remembered once when Spassky failed.

"I spent 20 minutes on my next move," Larsen said of this position.

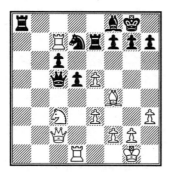

Larsen – Spassky

Montreal 1979

White to move

"For the first ten minutes, Spassky sat quietly at the board, but then he suddenly stood up and realized that he had overlooked something."

That alerted Larsen and he saw **22 ♖xd5!** was stronger than he had thought.

He won after **22...cxd5 23 ♖xc5 ♞xc5 24 ♞xd5**.

443. Is there something I should do when I reach the time control?

Experienced players say the two most important moves of a game are the very first move and the first move after a time control ends.

When the control ends, after you've been short of time, there is a danger of moving quickly, out of momentum.

The answer to your question: Take a deep breath and calm down.

444. How should I play against a much stronger player?

Be active. "If you play like Mr. Passive, we welcome that," said Larry Christiansen, a veteran of crushing many Mr. Passives.

Both players fear losing in a game, but a stronger player also fears the third result. So, if you want to draw with him, play as if you were trying to win:

Don't go out of your way to simplify. He is probably better than you in all phases but especially in the endgame.

Also, invite complications. If the position becomes so complex that neither of you knows what is really happening, you have made the playing field a bit more level. A master wants to beat you with routine moves. He does not want to try to calculate the incalculable.

And don't invent a new opening. A stronger player knows the major ones better than you. But the major ones are much sounder than something you thought up today.

445. What if I am the stronger player?

If you are much stronger, you might be able to blow him off the board with tactics in the opening or middlegame.

But if you are merely somewhat stronger, it pays to build up your winning chances slowly. The reason is arithmetic.

A weaker player is more likely to make a mistake than you. The longer the game, the greater the likelihood of that happening. Even if he errs only once every 10 moves, you have a better chance in a 50-move game than in a 30-move game.

446. Are there psychological tricks players use?

Many. There are legitimate as well as ethically-dubious kinds of gamesmanship.

Among the latter is a fake expression of dismay. In scholastic tournaments, young players will set a tactical trap and then play-act as if they had blundered.

Grandmasters are not above such theatrics. GM Gata Kamsky repeatedly tried this ploy during a match leading to the world championship. Several times he shook his head after making a move. "I would first look for a trap," said his opponent, Vishy Anand. "And several times I found one."

When some crafty masters got a lost position, they intentionally got into very bad time trouble. Their hope is their opponents will try to exploit the clock by making their own moves quickly and blunder.

There are many examples of bad manners. For example, young players who hope to claim the 50-move rule start counting the moves out loud.

447. What about the more polite ploys?

In an endgame some players will find their previously captured queen and place it more conveniently near the board. They are hinting that they will make a new queen and that it is time for their opponent to resign.

448. *Is there bluffing in chess?*

Indeed, there is. There are no hidden cards, but there is a lot of uncertainty. A tricky opponent can use that to bluff.

Kamsky – Svidler

World Cup 2011

White to move

Several moves earlier, Black realized he had blundered. After studying the position briefly he "decided to play very quickly, pretending that I had everything under control."

White responded by making second-best moves. The result was this double-edged position. White blundered with **26 ♘xb8??** and was lost after **26...♖e2!** (27 ♕xe2 ♕g3! and mates).

He had no way to protect his queen and also f2. He resigned after **27 ♕c3 ♖xf2 28 ♘c6 ♖xf1+**.

After playing a world championship, David Bronstein was asked what he discovered about his opponent. "Most of all, what I learned from [Mikhail] Botvinnik was his knowledge of how to bluff," he said.

Chapter Twenty Three: Tournaments

449. Are there separate tournaments for men and women?

What most people think of as men's tournaments are actually open to all players. Because so few women enter some of them, it seems like they are men-only.

450. But aren't there women-only tournaments?

Yes. Some women strongly support them as a way of encouraging women to earn large cash prizes. Other women refuse to play in them because they want the opportunity to improve and their best opportunities are playing men.

It's a controversial issue and there have been women who were on one side and then the other.

451. Are there tournaments limited to the very young or the elderly?

Yes, they range from under-8 tournaments up.

The World Senior Championship is divided into four sections, for over-50 and over-65, with separate open and women-only sections. Nona Gaprindashvili, a former World Women's Champion won the over-65 women's title at age 77.

452. How many different world champions are there?

In over-the-board chess, 16 different world champions based on age are crowned in a typical year. There are also world championships in special categories, such as for composing and solving problems and studies.

453. Can you play out of your age group?

A youngster can enter a tournament designated for older juniors. A senior over 65 can play in an over-50 tournament.

Rameshbabu Praggnanandhaa of India won the world under-8 championship when he was seven. A year later he entered and played well in the world under-20 championship. Here is one of his games from the tournament.

Praggnanandhaa – Pastar

Pune 2014

1 e4 c5 2 ♘f3 e6 3 ♘c3 a6 4 a4 ♘c6 5 ♗e2 d5 6 exd5 exd5 7 d4 c4 8 0-0 ♗f5 9 ♖e1 ♗e7 10 ♗f4 ♘f6 11 ♗xc4! dxc4 12 d5 ♘b4?

Black would only be slightly worse after 12...0-0 13 dxc6 bxc6.

13 d6 ♗xc2 14 ♕d2 ♘g8

White to move

15 ♘d5! ♘d3 16 ♘c7+ ♔f8 17 dxe7+ ♘xe7 18 ♘xa8 ♘d5 19 ♕xc2 ♘5xf4 20 ♕xc4 ♕xa8 21 ♖ed1 ♘e2+ 22 ♔f1 ♘df4 23 ♘e5 resigns

Praggnanandhaa became a grandmaster four years later.

454. What happens in a tournament if there is a breach of the rules and neither player complains?

The game goes on. As noted in Question 374, some rules are optional.

Nakamura – Kasparov

St. Louis 2016

Black to move

The former world champion played 26...♘b4 but then saw 27 ♗c5!.

There was little doubt his hand had left the knight but he immediately changed his move to **26...♘f4**.

White could have insisted on the blunder standing, under the touch-move rule. He did not and the game went on. It was eventually drawn.

455. How is it determined who plays whom in a tournament?

There are different formats for pairing. Three of them are the most popular – the round robin, the knockout and the Swiss system. Each has its plusses and minuses.

456. What is a round robin?

It is also called all-play-all – and that explains it pretty well.

Each player is paired with every other player. The order in which they face one another is usually determined by a drawing of lots before the tournament begins.

The number of rounds is determined by the number of players. If there are 12 players, each plays 11 rounds. A variation of this is a "double round robin." Each player faces each other player twice, once as White and once as Black.

A major benefit of a round robin is no one is eliminated, as in a knockout tournament.

457. How does a knockout work?

In the most common version, called "single elimination," a player is knocked out of the tournament when he loses a game.

His opponent advances to the next round. Additional players are knocked out in each successive round until there are two players are left. The winner of their game takes first prize.

The first international tournament, London 1851, was held on a knockout basis. One of the pre-tournament favorites was Howard Staunton. But he never reached the finals because he was knocked out earlier by another favorite, Adolf Anderssen.

Anderssen – Staunton

London 1851

1 e4 e5 2 ♘f3 ♘c6 3 d4 exd4 4 ♗c4 ♗c5 5 0-0 d6 6 c3 ♘f6 7 cxd4 ♗b6 8 ♘c3 ♗g4 9 ♗e3 0-0 10 a3 ♕e7 11 ♕d3 ♗xf3 12 gxf3 ♕d7 13 ♔g2 ♘h5 14 ♘e2 ♘e7 15 ♘g3 ♘xg3 16 hxg3 d5 17 ♗a2 ♖ad8 18 ♖ad1 c6 19 ♖h1 ♘g6 20 ♖h5 dxe4 21 fxe4 ♕g4! 22 ♖dh1 ♖xd4 23 ♕c3 ♖xe4 24 ♖xh7 ♗d4! 25 ♗xd4

Black to move

With 25...♘f4+! 26 ♔g1 ♛d1+ and ...♛xd4, Staunton would have had the better winning chances.

But after he blundered with **25...♖xd4??** he lost his queen, **26 ♖1h4! ♘xh4+ 27 ♖xh4 ♛xh4**, and the game.

Anderssen advanced to the final round, in which he won the unofficial title of world champion.

458. What is the Swiss System?

This is an attempt to improve on the round robin and knockout.

No one is knocked out. The winner of a game is awarded one point, the loser gets a zero and they each receive a half point in case of a draw.

Then in the next round, players are paired against opponents with the same score.

459. What are the benefits and drawbacks of the three tournament formats?

The Swiss system is the most flexible. It allows an unlimited number of participants of varying strengths to compete.

It is common for an open tournament using Swiss pairings to have more than 100 players. A round-robin with 100 players would mean each would have to play an impossible 99 games.

The number of players in a knockout is more or less limited to factors of two. That is, 4, 8, 16, 32, 64 and 128 players. The number of rounds is also limited: It takes six rounds for 128 players to be reduced to two finalists, for instance.

The number of rounds in a Swiss tournament is not limited. But there is a possibility that a clear winner may not be determined. For example, if 100 players compete for six rounds, two players may finish in a tie with perfect 6-0 scores.

A complicating factor for a knockout is draws. They have to be broken each round of a single-elimination tournament to determine who is knocked out.

460. Why aren't there separate tournaments for professionals and amateurs the way there are in some sports?

The principal difference between pro and amateur sports tournaments is the large prize funds for the pros. Amateur tournaments in some sports offer little or no cash prizes.

In chess, there are professional events in all but name. These are invitational grandmaster tournaments. Top players can earn tens of thousands of dollars in a first prize, as well as receiving a discreet appearance fee. There have been grandmaster tournaments in which the appearance fees exceeded the prize money.

The most popular events for amateurs are open tournaments using Swiss system pairings. Amateurs usually pay substantial entrance fees. Pros may also play in them and compete with one another for large first prizes, provided by the entrance fees.

461. Is there an element of luck in some of these formats?

There is some luck in all of them.

In a knockout, you can be paired with a strong opponent in one of the first rounds and be eliminated, while your friends face weaker opponents than you. That is what happened to Staunton in Question 457.

In a round robin with an even number of players, half of them will get an extra game with White and the others an extra Black. Vladimir Kramnik said this is worth a half point at the elite level.

Another luck factor is which players you face with which color. In a Swiss or round robin, the luck of the draw can give someone White against the stronger players and Black against the weaker ones, or vice versa.

Bobby Fischer registered his breakthrough success, at Bled 1961, thanks to scoring 3½-½ against the Soviet players. Mikhail Botvinnik attributed this to his "luck" in having White against all four of his countrymen.

Fischer – Petrosian

Bled 1961

Black to move

Black should have no difficulty holding a draw after 35...♔c7.

But the game ended **33...♖xh3? 34 ♖b8+ ♔c7 35 ♖b7+ ♔c6?? 36 ♔c4!**. Black resigned before he was mated by, for example, 37 ♖e7.

There is also luck in the order in which you face opponents.

In a round robin, if you draw the right number (usually 1) you can get the White pieces in the first two rounds.

Also, in a round robin, players who are not in contention for a prize may be less combative in the last rounds.

Pairings in a Swiss system tournament have been criticized for their arbitrary nature. But today they are determined by computer programs such as "Swiss Manager."

462. What are the most common time controls?

Until the 21st century, the most popular time limit by far was a slow one, such as 40 moves in two or two and a half hours. This became known as the "classical" control, after faster formats became popular.

The two main fast controls are "rapid," which is more than 10 minutes for an entire game, and "blitz," which is shorter, such as five or seven minutes for an entire game.

Today there are world championships in all three controls but the "classical" is considered the one that determines the world's best player.

463. Why are there different time controls?

Convenience and the preference of players.

Speed tournaments last a few days, not the two or more weeks of a "classical" tournament.

A World Blitz Championship lasting 21 rounds was over in just two days in 2019. The World Rapid Championship that year lasted 15 rounds over three days. Here is how the tournament winner breezed through the second round.

Carlsen – Belov

World Blitz Championship 2019

1 e4 c6 2 d4 d5 3 exd5 cxd5 4 ♗d3 ♘c6 5 c3 ♘f6 6 ♗f4 ♗g4 7 ♕b3 ♕d7 8 ♘d2 e6 9 ♘gf3 ♗d6 10 ♘e5 ♕c7 11 0-0 0-0 12 ♖ae1 ♗h5 13 ♗g3 ♗g6 14 ♘xg6 hxg6 15 ♘f3 ♖ab8 16 ♕c2 ♖fc8 17 ♕e2 ♘e7 18 ♗xd6 ♕xd6 19 ♘e5 ♘f5 20 g4! ♘e7 21 f4 a6 22 ♕g2 b5

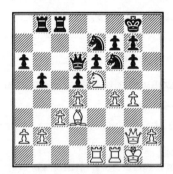

White to move

The pawn structure is so favorable to White that he has a choice of winning plans, including 23 ♖e3 and 24 ♖h3.

23 f5! exf5 24 gxf5 ♘xf5 25 ♗xf5 gxf5 26 ♖xf5 b4 27 ♖ef1 ♔f8? 28 ♖g5! bxc3 29 ♖xg7 cxb2 30 ♖xf7+ ♔e8 31 ♕g6 resigns

464. Should I be just as good at different time controls?

Only the professionals are equally skillful at blitz, rapid and classical.

They have plenty of practice today because they compete regularly in all three popular controls. Previously, the best players varied quite a bit in strength. Alexander Alekhine was known to be a poor blitz player. Mikhail Botvinnik refused to play at quick speeds. And he never got to play with the Fischer clock.

465. What is the Fischer clock?

It is a digital clock, patented by Bobby Fischer, based on the premise that each player will gain a small amount of time (an "increment") after he moves.

In this way, a player will never find himself with only two or three seconds in which to play several moves.

A tournament will list its time control, such as "30/90, 30 second increment." This means each player is allotted 90 minutes to play his first 30 moves but is given an extra 30 seconds each time he makes a move.

After Fischer used it in his 1992 rematch with Boris Spassky this format gained popularity. Today most tournaments use a version of the Fischer clock, usually with a time delay.

466. What is time delay?

This tweaks the Fischer format by preventing a player from adding extra minutes to his clock by making a series of quick moves and saving the unused portion of the increment.

In a 10-second time delay tournament, for example, a player's clock will not begin running until 10 seconds have expired. There is no increment for him to save.

467. What is sudden death?

When a Swiss tournament game lasts longer than others in a round it can delay the next round because the pairings depend on it.

A popular solution is to set a limit. The tournament regulations may give the base time controls, such as "40/2" – meaning 40 moves in two hours. Then it adds "SD/1".

This means after the initial control, each player gets one more hour to complete the game. They get to keep any unused time from the initial two hours.

The chief alternative to sudden death is adjudication.

468. What is that?

At some point in a long-running game, play is halted. A neutral third party steps in and plays the role of arbitrator. This person, usually a master, can declare the result: a win for one player or a draw.

Adjudication is controversial because there is wide variation in how to determine a win. Some adjudicators tend to declare a game is a draw unless there is a forced win. Others say it is a win if it is a "matter of technique."

469. What is a post-mortem?

This is the traditional way that two players will share their thoughts, after their game has ended, by reviewing their moves to see what they did right and did wrong.

There is no obligation to do this and many young players refuse an invitation to post-mortem if they lost. Some players think they will get all the answers by plugging the game moves into their computers.

470. What happens if there is a tie for first place?

The best way to break a tie is a playoff, of one or more games.

Ties are often a problem in a Swiss System. The two – or more – players in the tie will likely have faced very different opponents and may have faced very different levels of difficulty.

The fairest way is to compute the average or total strength of the opponents. There are various ways of doing this and the system that is used will be announced before the tournament begins.

In recent years, a playoff game using Armageddon rules has become a popular alternative to arithmetic tie-breaking.

471. What is Armageddon?

A single game at a quick time control but with the key provision that Black receives "draw odds."

That is, he is declared the winner of the playoff if he wins the game or draws it.

As compensation for this, White starts the game with more time. A common set of rules provides six minutes for White and five for Black.

Curiously, there is no consensus on whether Armageddon finishes favor White or Black.

Chapter Twenty Four: **Ratings and Titles**

472. How do I get a numerical rating?

Playing in an over-the-board tournament will get you the most widely recognized rating.

There are also Web sites that rate games at various speeds. On the Internet Chess Club, for example, you can get a rating for your one-minute games, another rating for three-minute games, for five-minute, 15-minute, and so on.

473. How does it work? Are my moves evaluated?

It has nothing to do with the quality of your moves, just the final result.

Each time you play a rated game your rating changes. If you win, you gain rating points. If you lose, you lose points.

Most rating systems operate on a zero-sum principle: The number of points you gain by beating an opponent will probably be the same as the number he loses.

474. How many points?

That is determined by the difference between your rating and your opponent's. The higher-rated the opponent, the more points you gain from a win.

Here is how 10-year-old Hikaru Nakamura set a record for the youngest player to defeat an international master. He was outrated by more than 400 points, so he gained the maximum. The quality of the moves didn't matter.

Nakamura – Bonin

New York 1997

1 e4 e6 2 d4 d5 3 e5 c5 4 c3 ♛b6 5 ♘f3 ♗d7 6 ♗e2 ♗b5 7 c4 ♗xc4 8 ♗xc4 dxc4 9 d5 exd5 10 ♛xd5 ♘e7 11 ♛xc4 ♛a6 12 ♘a3 ♛xc4 13 ♘xc4 ♘f5 14 a4 ♘c6 15 0-0 h6 16 ♗e3 0-0-0 17 ♖ad1 ♗e7 18 g4 ♘fd4 19 ♗xd4 cxd4 20 ♘fd2 h5 21 gxh5 ♖xh5 22 f4 f6 23 ♘f3 g5 24 exf6 ♗xf6 25 fxg5 ♗xg5 26 ♘xg5 ♖xg5+ 27 ♔h1 d3 28 b3 ♘e5 29 ♘b2 ♖g4 30 ♖fe1 ♖d5 31 ♖e3 d2 32 ♖e2 ♘f3 33 ♖f2 ♖f4? 34 ♘c4! ♖d3 35 ♘xd2

Black to move

Black's advantage disappeared in the last few moves. (A draw would be likely after 35...♔d7 36 ♖df1! ♘xd2 37 ♖xf4 ♘xf1).

That would be a very creditable result for a 10-year-old. But the game ended with **35...♖fd4?? 36 ♖c1+! resigns.**

475. What happens if I draw?

The lower-rated player gains points and the higher-rated player loses the same number. Again, zero-sum.

476. Can I gain more points by drawing a game than I would from winning against another opponent?

Yes, and this is fair.

Drawing with a master should be rewarded more highly than beating a very weak player.

477. Would I lose my rating if I don't play for a while?

No. Generally, you can keep a rating indefinitely. There is no penalty for inactivity.

478. Do ratings predict results?

Yes, despite the frequency of upsets.

The Elo rating system estimates that if your rating is 50 points higher than your opponent, you have a 57 percent chance of beating him.

If the difference is 100 points in your favor, that goes up to 64 percent. For a 200-point difference, it is 76 percent.

The greater the number of games, the more accurate the prediction. For instance, if you played a match of 10 games, the ratings would likely be much better in predicting the final score than if you played four games.

479. Can players from different generations be compared?

Yes – if you add an asterisk.

Magnus Carlsen became the highest-rated player in history, with a peak of 2882. He replaced Garry Kasparov, who had been the record-holder when he reached 2851. And Kasparov replaced Bobby Fischer, who had peaked at 2785.

The asterisk is appropriate because there has been inflation in ratings.

There were four players rated 2650 or higher in 1990, 27 in 1999 and nearly 100 in 2021. By 2021 Fischer was barely in the top 20 of highest rated players in history.

480. Isn't that because today's players are simply better? After all, they were able to train with computers.

Perhaps. But Mikhail Tal was the world's best player in 1960. Yet he didn't reach his peak rating until 1980.

At that time he could have given big material odds to the best programs. There was little he could have learned from engines.

Another example is Anatoly Karpov. He dominated the world's elite in the late 1970s and was world champion until 1985.

Yet he reached his peak rating in 1994, when he was 43. Machines could learn from him, not vice versa.

Karpov – Deep Thought

Cambridge 1990

Black to move

If Black gets his rook behind his passed pawn it can draw, 59...h3! 60 ♖xh6 a3 61 ♖xh3 ♖a4!.

But the game went **59...h5?? 60 ♔e5! h3 61 f5!** and Karpov was winning.

The rest was **61...♔g8 62 ♖xh5 a3 63 ♖xh3 a2 64 ♖a3 ♖c5+ 65 ♔f6 resigns**.

481. What is the range in ratings?

Fom lowest to highest it is nearly 3000 points.

Arpad Elo, who designed the most popular rating system, wanted to make sure that no one would ever have a negative number for a rating. As a result, there is a US rating category that starts at zero and goes up to 200.

At the other extreme are US players rated up to 2900. The median ratings fall around 1200 to 1400.

On the Internet Chess Club, the highest ratings have been over or close to 3000. This is at the fastest speeds.

482. How strong is a master?

A rating of over 2200. In the US, a "senior master" is someone rated over 2400. From 2000 to 2200 there is another title, expert.

483. Can you lose a title?

Yes, national master titles based on rating may be lost if your rating falls below 2200.

International titles are not based on fluctuating ratings and are permanent.

484. What are the international titles?

There are lifetime titles awarded by the world chess federation, known by its French acronym FIDE.

The highest is International Grandmaster. Below that is International Master and FIDE Master.

There are more 1700 grandmasters in the world.

485. If I learn more about chess, can I expect my rating to keep rising?

Don't expect a steady rise.

Mark Dvoretsky, one of the greatest ever chess teachers, said his students typically went through alternating periods of spurts and times when their rating didn't grow.

Walter Browne said he made his fastest progress from age 13 to 14. He became a master a year later and a grandmaster soon after that.

Howard – Browne

Seattle 1966

1 d4 d5 2 c4 dxc4 3 e3 ♘f6 4 ♗xc4 e6 5 ♘c3 ♘bd7 6 ♘f3 a6 7 0-0 c5 8 a3 cxd4 9 ♘xd4 b5 10 ♗a2 ♕b6 11 ♘f3 ♗b7 12 ♖e1 ♗e7 13 b4 0-0 14 ♗b2 ♖fd8 15 ♕e2 ♖ac8 16 ♖ad1 ♗xf3 17 ♕xf3 ♘e5 18 ♖xd8+ ♕xd8 19 ♕e2 ♕d3! 20 f4? ♕xe2 21 ♖xe2 ♘d3 22 ♗a1 ♘e4! 23 ♖c2 ♗f6! White resigns

Final position

Even for future grandmasters their spurts were followed by a period of plateauing.

486. What is plateauing?

It means your rating doesn't go up or down for a period of time.

There is a school of thought that says that once you begin playing in tournaments you reach a "natural" plateau.

"At some stage you're always going to hit a level that you can't really improve on without work," Grandmaster Michael Adams said.

Joel Benjamin, another grandmaster, recalled how he became a US expert at 11. This was a splendid achievement at the time. Expectations ran high that he would quickly progress to grandmaster. But he remained an expert for two years. "I don't know what happened at the end of two years but suddenly I was playing at the master level."

He became a grandmaster at 22. Even if you aspire to reach the top of Mount Everest there will be unexpected stops during the ascent.

Chapter Twenty Five: Miscellany

487. Why are some moves considered beautiful?

Several criteria have been suggested to weigh chess aesthetics. One common thread is "hard to foresee."

A sacrifice is considered pretty if it is unexpected. The more it challenges logical expectations, the greater the aesthetic effect. "The glowing power of a sacrifice is irresistible," as Rudolf Spielmann said.

488. What is a brilliancy prize?

An award offered for playing the prettiest game in a tournament.

The usual requirement is a sacrifice that appears risky but turns out to be sound. The longer that its soundness is uncertain helps. Today, if a computer does not quickly appreciate its soundness, this is a plus.

Some tournaments offer a separate "best-played game" prize.

489. Can one move make a game brilliant?

Yes, a single spectacular move can.

In some positions there can be more than one move with the same stunning tactical idea. Here's an example of a brilliancy prize move that could have been much better.

Pillsbury – Wolf

Monte Carlo 1903

White to move

White played **27 ♕xb6** and won the brilliancy prize based on the routine combination 27...♕xb6 28 ♗xh7+ and ♖xb6.

But 27 e6! is prettier and mates in four moves.

So does 27 ♘e6!, a line-closing tactic (27 …♖xe6 28 ♗xh7+ ♘xh7 29 ♖g4+).

490. Can humans compete with computers today?

No. The strongest programs are rated over 3500. This indicates they would score 98 percent of the time against the best human.

491. When did they become our superiors?

The 1997 match that Deep Blue won from Garry Kasparov was the event that got the most attention.

But the series of computer-versus-human matches continued after that. They were effectively ended when an engine named Hydra defeated Michael Adams by 5½-½ in 2005.

International Master David Levy, who had beaten computers earlier in highly publicized stakes matches, said the spectator interest in such exhibitions was disappearing because "the gladiator will always be beaten by the lion."

492. Are there variants of chess I can play with the same board and pieces?

Quite a few. Chess as we know it is a variant of the version that was played before 1500.

One reason that "our" game became accepted is that it used the same 8x8 square board and the same pieces as its predecessor. There was no reason to buy new equipment.

493. What is the most popular variant?

Today it is Fischerandom, also known as Fischer random and Chess 960.

Before the game begins, the placement of the first-rank pieces are chosen by lot. The two sides have the same basic placement. If White's queen begins at c1, Black's queen will start at c8.

There are 960 different ways the eight pieces can be placed. Bobby Fischer's role was to propose a version of it in 1996.

Long before that there were experimental tournaments that began with the position of the knights and bishops reversed.

494. What were the popular variants before Fischerandom?

It is not an actual variant but the most popular alternative to a traditional game was handicap chess – that is, games played at odds.

Before a game, a better player removed one or more of his pieces and pawns. This helped equalize the winning chances between opponents of different strengths.

The most common odds was "pawn and move." The odds giver took the Black pieces and removed his f-pawn. In about half of his surviving games, André Philidor gave "pawn and move."

There are also much greater handicaps, including knight odds, rook, odds and queen odds. This does not mean the odds-giver is a master. Winston Churchill, who was not known for his chess skill, said he gave queen odds to his son Randolph and won easily.

495. Are there variants of chess that require more than one board and set of pieces?

Yes, several. One is called Basque chess: The two players make moves on two adjacent boards. Each player has White on one board and Black on the other.

This can also be played with two clocks to add a new kind of strategy: Do you spend more time thinking about the game you might win or about the one you are trying to draw?

Another variant is called Bughouse chess. It has the same setup as Basque – two nearby boards and two clocks. The difference is that there are two players sitting side by side and playing as a team. One member of the team has White and the other has Black.

The key element is that when a player captures a piece, say a Black knight, he gives it to his teammate, who has the Black pieces next to him. The teammate can then place the knight anywhere on the board as his next move. The game continues until someone is mated or loses on time.

There are variants of chess using three boards.

496. How are they played?

One is a larger version of Bughouse, with three players on each team. The player on the middle board, say playing Black, can pass the White pieces he captured to either teammate.

Another three-board game is called Kriegspiel. In the most popular version, the third board is controlled by an umpire who makes the moves on it that are made by the two players on their boards.

But the two players, one playing White and the other playing Black, can only see their own pieces. They have to guess where their opponent's pieces are. When each player makes a move, the umpire determines whether it is legal on the third board. If it is, he makes it on that board and notifies the players whether it made a check or a capture.

497. Are there versions of chess using computers?

Advanced chess, also known as Centaur chess, allows players to consult their computers during a game.

The premise is that this provides for the highest quality of play, based on human intuition and computer calculation. During the brief period of interest in Centaur chess, the evidence of a higher level of play was not evident in the games, like this.

Kramnik – Anand

Leon 2002

Black to move

Playing quickly, the computer was little help to Black and he lost after **25...♛b6? 26 ♕g4 ♗f4? 27 ♘d5 ♕d8 28 ♘xf4 exf4 29 d7.**

The premise lost its allure when it became clear that computers were much better than humans. They no longer needed our input to find the best move.

498. Is correspondence chess still played?

Sending moves by mail has largely ceased. But correspondence chess exists in other forms. Moves are transmitted by email or on turn-based Web sites. They vary in terms of whether they allow players to consult computers. Some correspondence players say they have continued to play Advanced chess this way.

499. Are there any variants with rules quite unlike those of normal chess?

Many. There is Checkless chess: No checks are allowed until checkmate.

Similar to that is No Castling chess. This alters the game much less than other variants.

A big change lies in Losing chess. You must capture if a capture is legal, but you can exercise a choice of captures. There are no checks or checkmate. The winner is the player who has only a king left – or, in another variant, nothing left because kings can be taken.

There are also multiple-move variants. In Marseilles chess, each player can make two moves in a row. In Progressive chess, White makes one move, then Black can make two, then White can play three and so on.

500. And finally, is chess in danger of being "solved"?

In theory, yes. But it will take a lot longer than many players once imagined.

Checkers was solved in 2007 when computers determined that with best play a game would be a draw. But checkers is played on only 32 squares and the pieces do not have the range of capability that chess does.

An indication of the difficulty is the progress in developing endgame tablebases. After decades of research, computers using tablebases can now play the best moves in positions with six pieces, and in some cases with seven pieces.

But 32 pieces? That's a mathematical problem no one is expected to solve in our lifetimes.

Index

(Numbers refer to questions. The bold face questions refer to games played by the subject players.)

Openings Index

(Numbers refer to questions).